WHEN A CHILD YOU LOVE IS GRIEVING

HAROLD IVAN SMITH

Beacon Hill Press of Kansas City
Kansas City, Missouri

Copyright 2004
Beacon Hill Press of Kansas City

ISBN 083-412-1735

Cover Art: Luke, age 9; his view of heaven, drawn after his grand-mother's death
Cover Design: Keith Alexander

Library of Congress Cataloging-in-Publication Data

Smith, Harold Ivan, 1947-
   When a child you love is grieving / Harold Ivan Smith.
      p. cm.
   Includes bibliographical references.
      ISBN 0-8341-2173-5 (pbk.)
   1. Bereavement in children—Religious aspects—Christianity. 2. Children and death—Religious aspects—Christianity. 3. Child rearing—Religious aspects—Christianity. I. Title.

   BV4596.P3S65 2004
   248.8'66—dc22

                                                      2004022122

10 9 8 7 6 5 4 3 2 1

CONTENTS

APPENDICES

"Let the little children grieve . . . and do not hinder them, for the kingdom of God belongs to such as these" (Luke 18:16, paraphrased).

INTRODUCTION

"Before you begin talking to your child about the death of a loved one or talking about death in general, be sure you know where you stand . . . You don't want your child's view of death to be shaped by any lingering inhibitions that you might have. The more you understand yourself, the easier it will be to avoid letting those feelings influence your child" (Helen Fitzgerald).[1]

Grieving children should be seen *and* heard.

The seed for this book may have been planted the morning after Christmas 1960. My maternal grandfather, Walter Eckert, died Christmas Eve—a most inappropriate time for a child's grandfather to die. That crisp, winter morning, the day after Christmas, the Eckert family gathered for the funeral. For some reason, all the grandsons sat together—in some ways a bad decision because the quartet of my grandfather's elderly friends started in the wrong key and took a while to find the correct key and tempo. I am not sure which cousin snickered first, but as all of us laughed, I thought, "There's going to be a second corpse. My dad is going to kill me!" Although I remember nothing of the funeral sermon, I remember that it was expected that every family member walk past the open casket for a final good-bye, then turn and walk up the center aisle of the funeral parlor and through the main door to the waiting cars that would take us to the cemetery.

Up to that moment, although a grandson missing Grandpa, I tried not to cry in front of my cousins. Then, at the casket, I began to sob. I stumbled up the aisle. As the funeral director opened the door, an adult stepped to my side and slipped her arm around me and hugged me. It was my Sunday School teacher, Hazel Bellebaum. She had never met my grandfather, but she had driven 30 miles to be there for the funeral and for a student in her class. In that moment she was there for me. Few times in my life have I felt as comforted. In fact, I am fighting tears sitting here at McDonald's as I recall and write about the experience.

I cannot remember how long I stood crying, but I do remember I felt safe as Mrs. Bellebaum repeatedly whispered, "It's OK, Harold. It's OK to cry." Her soft but firm voice was so comforting.

I was a sensitive child—overly sensitive. I was a big sissy in the eyes of some of my athletically inclined cousins and uncles. "Always got his nose stuck in some book!" I had so wanted to appear strong in front of my cousins that day. But, as commonly happens, grief ambushed me.

One Sunday School teacher made a huge difference for 0a young boy that sad morning after Christmas. She worked as a bookkeeper in a women's store. I doubt that she had ever had a course in grief counseling. Her example of immediate compassionate care for a child was imprinted on my heart and memory.

I am reasonably sure that I never thanked Mrs. Bellebaum. Maybe this book will serve as a belated thank-you.

Unfortunately, not all children have a Hazel Bellebaum in their lives, in their griefs. Arthur, age six, withdrew from life emotionally after his mother died. After witnessing his father's anguished mourning, the child did not dare ask questions that might upset his father. Tennis provided an escape. Arthur later recalled:

> I don't remember grieving over my mother. She died, and life moved on. My father told people how my response to the news, as he sat crying his eyes out between my brother Johnnie and me, was simply enough. "Don't cry, Daddy," I consoled him. "As long as we have each other, we'll be all right." I don't remember any of that.[2]

Not surprisingly, over the years, Arthur developed a reputation as aloof. Some colleagues conjectured that the aloofness was influenced by Mattie's death and by the death of Arthur's grandfather within a 12-month period, two significant losses for a six-year-old.

> I have understood that this quality of emotional distance in me . . . may very well have something to do with the ear-

8

ly loss of my mother. I have never thought of myself as having been cheated by her death, but I am terribly, insistently, aware of an emptiness in my soul that only she could have filled.[3]

As a compassionate care-er you can make a difference, one grieving child at a time. I doubt that as Mrs. Bellebaum gathered up her purse that morning she said, "I will need to be ready to be compassionate this morning." Simply, she just showed up in a funeral home for a funeral for a stranger.

The child you touch, hug, comfort today may never say thank you. But God notices such acts of compassion and caring. Jesus modeled an incredibly high standard when He allowed His ministry to be interrupted by children. From experience, Andy Lester concludes:

It is clear to anyone who works in depth with people that crises in childhood can cause problems for people in their teens and youth years: unresolved grief, unnecessary fears, lacks of trust, loss of self-esteem, and distorted ideas about the character of God and how God works in the world. It is also apparent that intervention by a committed, caring minister can enable children to pass through crises with a strengthened sense of self, renewed trust in their coping skills, and a firmer faith in God-who-is-love.[4]

PART I

AUDIT your own grief experience

"Children are people experiencing life, not just getting ready for it" (William C. Kroen).[1]

"To help children in this process, we must confront our own fears and begin to search for the words that we do not have" (Phyllis Silverman).[2]

When you talk to a child about grief, at least four individuals are represented in the conversation: the child, you, the child's deceased, and your dead. Before we examine practical caring acts, it is important to reassess your experience with an awareness of grief. As a potential care-er, you need to reflect on three questions developed by noted nurse educators Priscilla LeMone and Karen Burke. You may want to, in the words of young adults, "hang out" with these questions—originally developed to help nurses confront grief issues:

- What are my personal feelings about how grief should be expressed?
- Am I making judgments about the meaning of loss to this [child]?
- Are unresolved losses in my own life preventing me from relating [caringly] to the child?[3]

Experience shapes response far into adulthood. Minnie Taylor, pregnant at age 50, had fallen down a circular staircase in her Texas home. Now as she lay in a rural hospital, dying, she asked to see her 5-year-old daughter, Claudia.

"She looked over at me," Claudia recalled, "and said, 'My poor little girl, her face is dirty.'" Minnie asked for a wet washcloth. Gently she scrubbed her child's face then fell back onto the bed and burst into tears, "Nobody at home to care for you but the Black nurse. Poor child." (Claudia's father ran a country store and worked long hours. He had no time for raising a child.)

Minnie Taylor died soon after her child left the hospital. At least Claudia, who in adult life was Lady Bird Johnson, knew that her mother had died. Minnie's husband chose not to tell his sons, Antonio and Tommy, away at boarding school, for almost a year. Antonio held that against his father for the rest of his life.[4] How could a father not tell a child that his mother had died?

Claudia was significantly impacted by her father's mourning after her mother died. Claudia had not been allowed to attend her mother's funeral. Days later when the minister paid a visit to the father and child, he commented that Minnie Taylor was "better off in heaven than on earth." Pointing at Claudia, Taylor angrily demanded, "Who's going to take care of that little girl!"[5]

Witnessing her father's rage, Claudia made up her mind not to be the burden he feared. "I just felt so sorry for him . . . I had no feelings at all for myself."[6] Indeed, many children can be so busy monitoring the mourning of others in the family—or physically or emotionally taking care of them—that they ignore their own grief.

During cotton picking season Taylor stayed at his general store 24 hours a day (or chose to stay as a defense against his grief). Many nights, he made a pallet for Claudia on the floor near the caskets he sold. One night as she went to sleep, Claudia asked, "What are those long boxes?" Taylor hesitated a moment and answered, "Dry goods, honey, just dry goods."

As a result of her father's insensitivity, the girl learned early on to keep her emotions buried, "symbolically locked in a coffin in her soul."[7] When school was out, Taylor sent Claudia by train to Minnie's family in Alabama. "He dressed her in a nice dress, tied a bonnet around her head, and put a sign around her neck, 'Deliver this child to John Will Pattillo'" (her great-uncle). Today that would constitute child abuse, but this six-year-old perceived the trip as an adventure. "I knew the conductors and porters would take care of me."[8] Unfortunately, because the Pattillo elders in Alabama warned Claudia's cousins not to talk about Minnie's death, she mourned in silence in her mother's extended family. Fortunately for the child—and the nation— that fall the child's aunt, Effie Pattillo, moved to Karmack to look after her.

What went through Lady Bird (Claudia Taylor) Johnson's mind in those early hours following the assassination of John Kennedy in 1963 when she observed and thought about six-year-old Caroline Kennedy? Did Mrs. Johnson remember her grief experience as a child-griever 45 years earlier? Did the loss she experienced then shape her compassion toward Caroline—especially the decision to allow Mrs. Kennedy and her children time to move out of the White House?

A young boy in Texas had not been told that his four-year-old sister could die while undergoing treatment for leukemia in New York City. At school one day he looked out the window and noticed his parents' car enter the parking lot. Good, he thought, they're home—meaning his parents *and* his sister. He had clearly seen three passengers in the car. Excused by his teacher, he excitedly dashed to the car. After getting in the car he was stunned: the back seat was empty!

"Where's Robin?" he asked.

"She died," his parents answered soberly.

No one had even hinted to this child that his sister could die. Suddenly, this boy had questions. He could not understand why his parents had not told him his sister would die. Weeks later, attending a high school football game with his dad, the boy grumbled that he wished he was with his sister.

"Why would you say that?" said his father, stunned by the comment.

"I bet she can see the game better from up there than we can from here."[9]

That seven-year-old was George W. Bush. Forty-six years after that incident, he reflected, "I am certain I saw her, her small head rising above the backseat of my parents' green Oldsmobile." He added, "Those moments remain the starkest memory of my childhood, a sharp pain in the midst of an otherwise happy blur."[10]

Somewhere, perhaps down the street, across the apartment complex, as you read this, given the 2.4 million deaths annually,[11] children are experiencing "sharp pain." Some childhoods will be forever altered. Not simply by the death of a loved one, but by the lack of attentive care focused on the child. And as you read this, some well-meaning soul will contend, "Oh, but children are so resilient." Or an adult will invade the child's grief space with a predetermined set of grief inhibitors:

"Your loved one is with Jesus in heaven."

"Your loved one is free of pain."

"Your loved one would want you to be a big boy."

"You have to be a big girl now!"

A child grieves in a culture determined that grievers, regardless of age, "move it along" or at least "accept" the death. My colleague, Ron Oliver, head of pastoral care at Norton's Kosair Hospital in Louisville, has seen numbers of children die, and says, "You do not *accept* a death. You accept the terms of a contract or conditions of employment. You do not accept death. It never becomes acceptable." One parent told Oliver, "I know she is dead. But I go to the window whenever a school bus goes by—just in case."[12]

Dexter King, looking back on his father's murder 40 years earlier, would agree. He writes soberly in his memoirs, "You never recover."[13] As Dexter and so many other children have learned, grief has a way of reannouncing its influence in a spiritual or psychological ambush years after the death. In a "get over it!" culture, Aaron Latham has lived with grief for his sister for years.

"I can tell you with certainty that the loss of a sibling leads to survivor guilt.

"Why her, not me? Wasn't she better than I am? And survivor guilt often leads in turn to callings . . . of one kind or another. A religious calling. A literary calling. A political calling. The calling is strong because you are, in a sense, living for two: You *have* to do well!"[14]

Many grievers make promises—and some keep the promises. Latham recalled, "As I was leaving the cemetery after my sister's burial 33 years ago, I promised: I'm going to write a book—something I had never done—and dedicate it to my sister. Within a year, I had done so."[15]

Latham devoured books on sibling loss and talked "endlessly

to psychiatrists." Personal experience shaped his research on the continuing impact of Robin Bush's death on her brother George. Latham insists that you do repeatedly revisit loss.

> Actually around 40 is when it usually happens. The real bite of survivor guilt clamps down around midlife. Or so I am told. I was 41 when it knocked me head over heels. You ask yourself what your sister would think of the use you have made of your life. The life she never had.[16]

Latham noted that George Bush's "spiritual awakening," took place at age 39. Latham asked Don Evans, the trusted friend of the president, "Do you think the loss of his sister had anything to do with Bush's religious awakening?"

"Sure. Certainly that's something he thinks about. Your Lord is who you look to in times of pain and suffering" or in what Latham terms, "ex post facto suffering."[17]

In some families, one surviving child, whatever the age, takes on the belief that he or she must now live out a parent's dreams for the dead child. That mumbled admonition, "You've got to be good . . ." ricochets permanently down the thought paths of the child. You mustn't lead your parents, by your choices, to conclude, "I wish he had been the one who died!"

After you read these questions developed by grief educator Helen Fitzgerald, spend some time pondering each question individually. You might write one question on the top of a page in a notebook and date your response. Then, from time to time, as you read this book, revisit your experience.

1. What is the earliest memory you have of a death?

2. How did you learn about this particular death?

3. How did you initially respond to this death?

4. Who protected you from the reality of death?

5. Did you go to the funeral home? Visitation? Funeral? Cemetery at the time of burial? Later?

6. How prepared were you for what you saw or experienced?

7. Who comforted you?

8. Who encouraged or discouraged your expression of emotions and feelings and fears?

9. Did you have to do anything that made you uncomfortable—such as touch or kiss the corpse?

10. How did your religious beliefs shape your experience with death?

11. How have you been impacted by this death?

12. As a child did you have any superstitions about death?

13. As you look back on the experience, what comes to mind?[18]

Spend some time reviewing other deaths you experienced as a child or adolescent. What have you learned from those losses?

John Kennedy said, just weeks before his death, "We can say with some assurance that, although children may be the victims of fate, they will not be the victims of our neglect."[19] What in your personal experience of grief—or absence of personal experience—led you to compassionate care or to neglect grieving children?

RECOGNIZE individuality

"Those poor children!" (Ethel Kennedy upon learning that John Kennedy had been assassinated).[1]

Maude Shaw, the Irish nanny for the Kennedy children who was given the responsibility of informing them of their father's death, anticipated differences in how the children would respond to the news. She also knew that there would be differences, because of the ages and emotional maturity, in how Caroline and John grieved.

It is important to recognize the individuality of children and the particularity of the responses to a death-event by siblings. Just as a six-year-old and a three-year-old will respond differently, not all six-year-olds will respond similarly. Norm Wright cautions, "A child in grief is a mystery. If you're looking for predictability, you may not find it."[2] This thumbnail overview of development framework for grieving children may be helpful.

Under age 2: A child has little understanding of death but does sense change in environment and security.

Theresa Huntley explains, "Children tend to experience their spiritual questioning as a disruption in their sense of security, stability, predictability, and fairness of life . . . Their original beliefs will either be affirmed and strengthened or adjusted in some way."[3] The child asks, "Who is going to be here for *me?*" The child realizes he or she needs adults to provide the basics of life.

Grief counselor Linda Goldman reminds us that age-groups are merely generalizations. Reactions may vary from child to child and from family to family.[4]

Ages 2 to 6: A child displays magical thinking.

"When will he come home?" Thus John Kennedy Jr., used to the dramatic arrivals of his father on a helicopter at the White House, asked Maude Shaw, "I wonder when he's coming back."[5] Hours after the assassination, many in the White House were moved to tears when John-John, hearing the helicopters, assumed his father was home and began enthusiastically shouting, "Daddy's home! Daddy's home!" (It was a presidential helicopter bearing the new president, Lyndon Johnson.)[6]

Ages 6 to 9: Children begin to comprehend the finality of death but often regress to magical thinking.

Allie Sims' baby brother Austin died when she was five years old. Five years later, one day in the kitchen, Allie broke down and began confessing her terrible secret.

"I killed my baby brother." Her mother was stunned. "What do you mean?"

A few weeks after Austin's birth, Allie, unthrilled by the loss of her status as center of the universe with her parents, had gone into Austin's room and said to him, "You can just go back where you came from!" When the child died of a brain tumor, given the "magical thinking" of a child, she assumed that she had caused his death.[7] Joy Johnson comments that magical thinking "reflects the feelings of power we either hope we have, wish we had, or are afraid we have."[8]

Whatever the age, children need to be told—and retold—that they did not do anything, say anything, or think anything that caused the child to die.

Children have long lists of "I wishes" following a significant loss. "I wish my mom could be here for my piano recital"—or soccer tournament—especially when parents and grandparents of peers will be visibly present.

Ages 9 to 10: Children acquire a more mature understanding of death and begin to appreciate its irreversibility.

Consider the impact of television, particularly cartoons. In one common theme, "an animal character is smashed or thrown off a cliff, in effect killed, only to bounce back to life in the next frame, looking no worse for the experience." Through repeated exposure to this, children come to "believe that death is reversible."[9]

Ages 11 to 14: A budding sense of invincibility filters death's menace.

Nevertheless, many children conclude, "Yes, it can happen—but not to *me* or to someone I love." Madeleine's family had fled Czechoslovakia 10 days after the Nazi army marched into Prague in March 1939. Madeleine recalls at age 8, "My parents told us they had learned that my grandparents had died during the war [World War II]." That is communicating a fact. "They said their parents had been old, and that's what happened when you got old." That is interpreting a fact.

After Hitler's defeat in 1945, Madeleine's father, a diplomat, was on the first plane back to Prague. Some weeks later, when his family joined him, Madeleine noticed that her mother cried often. When asked, her mother would only say, "It's just that I am so glad to be back home."[10]

Years later, on her first day as Secretary of State in January 1997, Madeleine Kobel Albright learned that her grandparents had died not because they were old but because they were Jews! They had died in a concentration camp. The last time Madeleine's mother saw her mother was when the grandmother had brought 2-year-old Madeleine back to Prague before they fled on a train to safety. Raised as a Christian, Madeleine now had to deal with her Jewish lineage.

Unfortunately, for Secretary Albright, the discovery was reported in a *Washington Post* article and then disseminated by the news media around the world. (The United States having a Jewish Secretary of State—a woman—was a political bombshell.) Soon, pundits were questioning how Madeleine Albright could *not* have known the fate of her grandparents. "One writer wondered why I hadn't asked to see the graves when informed as an 8-year-old that my grandparents were dead. The clear insinuation was that I was a liar."[11]

I had learned of my grandparents' deaths . . . upon my family's return to Prague after World War II. I felt sorry for my parents but did not grieve myself because I didn't really know what grandparents were. I couldn't picture their faces or remember their smiles or imagine their arms around me.

22

I was less than two years old when I had last seen them, so I had little curiosity about them. I knew old people die.[12]

Reading these thumbnail concepts, hopefully you can anticipate and appreciate the differences, based on age development, within a family of, say, four children. Moreover, one must ask what children learn from siblings or other children or tell each other. John never has forgotten being shamed for crying at his father's funeral. "My brother leaned down and snarled, 'Don't be such a big baby! Big boys don't cry.'"

There is a wonderful story about Bobby Kennedy, after the death of John's father, spending an afternoon trying to teach John-John how to kick a football. After each kick, John fell to the ground. His Uncle Robert, serving as surrogate father, snapped, "Get up! Try it again!" After the sixth or seventh time, however, little John would not get up off the ground.

"Come on, a Kennedy never gives up," Bobby chided.

John responded, "Humph, here's one that does."[13]

Children may feel enormous pressure to be a "big boy" or a "big girl" or to be "Mama's little man" after a death. So, they disassociate themselves from developmental norms to fulfill the new expectation. Alan Wolfelt will not tolerate this pressuring. "Boys are not men and shouldn't be expected to take on adult roles. If someone is pressuring a grieving boy to 'be a man,' maybe you can intervene and take some of the heat off." He adds, "'Being strong' in grief just means postponing normal thoughts and feelings, complicating the child's life and compromising his happiness for years to come."[14]

Biographer Richard Klein commented on the life of Aristotle Onassis, whose mother died when the boy was six, "The early loss of his mother was, most likely, the source of his lifelong melancholy and of the deep insecurities that he always sought to cover up."[15]

Elizabeth Hutchinson Jackson died of typhus in 1781, leaving a 13-year-old son, Andrew. A biographer writes:

> Betty had been the most important person in her son's life—the person who had advised him, admired him, believed in him, encouraged him, protected him against ene-

mies. No one else . . . could fill those roles. He would revere her memory and cite her as an authority as long as he lived.

Certain consequences of her death radiated through the rest of [Andrew] Jackson's life. The reverence he felt for his mother he would extend to women in general.[16]

If Andrew Jackson Sr. had not died days before his son's birth, if Betty Jackson had not died when Andrew was 13, would he have become the Andrew Jackson of destiny? (In fact, three U.S. presidents were born after their fathers' deaths: Rutherford B. Hayes, Andrew Jackson, and Bill Clinton; John Tyler was 7 when his mother died, Abraham Lincoln was 9, Calvin Coolidge was 12.)

In this culture some children have been exposed to so much death and loss that they may not exhibit traditional age developmental norms. Many children have seen parents, grandparents, siblings, friends, or neighbors die in traffic accidents or homicides or disasters. Imagine the long-term affects in Africa where an estimated 12 million children have been orphaned by AIDS, or the 12,000 AIDS orphans in Guatemala.[17] Those children carry significant emotional baggage that will shape their adulthoods.

There is, however, a flip side to early exposure to significant loss. Sherwin Nuland, distinguished professor of medicine at Yale and the author of the best-seller *How We Die*, attributes his decision to study medicine to his mother's illness and death.

My mother died of colon cancer one week after my 11th birthday, and that fact has shaped my life. All that I have become and much that I have not become, I trace directly or indirectly to her death . . . In my professional and personal life, I have lived with the awareness of death's imminence for more than half a century.[18]

What might Nuland have become had his mother lived?

I have wondered what must have gone through the mind of Herbert after the deaths of his mother and father before age 10. Herbert was sent from his farm near West Branch, Iowa, to live with an aunt and uncle on an Indian reservation in Oklahoma. Not only did he lose his parents, but he also lost the sense of familiar surroundings and friends and his church. Later, he was sent to live in Oregon with an aunt and uncle he did not know. Those losses, however, shaped his compassion during his work as a humanitarian for Europe's orphans and hungry children following World War I—an experience that propelled him toward the presidency. Could he have been such a driven humanitarian had he not experienced being an orphan? Herbert Hoover, orphan, was elected president of the United States in 1928.[19]

At a time when peers are preoccupied with dogs and soccer, math and computers, a grieving child must struggle with the brutal reality that someone important to him or her has died and the family has changed. This child has to ask, "Am I going to die?" or, to caring adults, "Are you going to die?" This child must deal with "Where is my loved one *now*?" And with the reality that "up in heaven" is not always a satisfactory answer. Consider children growing up in families with no religious beliefs or whose key adults do not believe in heaven. What would you tell this child?

Adults should have three primary goals in working with a grieving child:

- To allow the child to put the event(s) into perspective
- To allow the child to make sense of the confusion
- To help the child begin to develop an understanding about death in general[20]

Children continually revise their understanding as they age. Sometimes to protect a child from the raw realities, some families edit the narrative of a particular death or hide details. However, at some point, the child must regrieve the loss based on the discovery of details that have been withheld.

Putting the events into perspective can be challenging for a child. You've heard, "Don't judge a man until you have walked in his shoes." Well, do not judge a child until you have walked in his or her sneakers.

Grief has three perspectives: initial, temporary, and long-term. As children age, they developmentally incorporate more details into a new or expanded understanding. In a sense, children work with details and feelings the way they work with a lump of clay—it is constantly shaped and reshaped.

I think the funeral rituals offer important opportunities for confronting reality and finality. Imagine a child's confusion when told that grandmother has died and there are no rituals. Grandmother is literally "here today and gone tomorrow."

When children are prepared for funeral rituals—by adults who are in touch with grief—they can have positive experiences for saying good-bye. Norm Wright notes that including children in planning funeral rituals can have a positive impact in their journeys toward reconciliation with the loss. "Children who are prepared for a funeral are better able to handle it than those who aren't given prior or accurate information. It helps them feel useful at a time when many are feeling overwhelmed."[21]

We do children no favors by camouflaging death. Peter Selwyn had been told as a child and young adult that his father had accidentally fallen from an office window when Peter was 18 months old.

> For my entire childhood, this was as much as I knew about him, his life, and his death. Because of the unusual circumstances of his death, this event and even the memory of his life quickly became family secrets that I was not permitted to discuss, so in effect, I experienced a double loss. In some ways, I had come to believe that maybe he had never existed. Moreover, as a child, whenever I asked, which was not very often, I was told that he had died in a fall from a window, that he had had poor balance, and that this was a terrible accident. I suppose that this seemed so bizarre that maybe I believed it was true; or else, given the way people's expressions and tones of voice would change whenever I brought it up, I got the message that this was not something that was acceptable to discuss. My mother would use an awkward, slightly disapproving tone when she used the phrase *your father,* which was the only way that I have ever heard her refer to him. There were no pictures of

him anywhere in the house, no mementoes—nothing to remind me or preserve the memory of this irreplaceable part of my life.[22]

In elementary school, the father's absence seemed "more painful, larger than it might have been otherwise" because Peter had not known him "long enough to have any conscious memories of him. I felt robbed of this past, not only by my surviving family, who seemed to want to suppress it, but also by him leaving so soon.[23] Only after becoming a prominent AIDS specialist at Yale with two children of his own did Peter Selwyn go back and revisit his quest for knowledge about his father. In his medical practice, as he watched fathers with children die, Selwyn began to acknowledge that he had "never come to terms with this first and primal loss."[24]

Reconstructing the story, piece by piece, despite many gaping holes, the scientist in Peter concluded that his father had died by suicide. When he asked if any other pictures existed, his mother produced a few old photos and a shoe box that she had stored in the top of a closet all those years. Inside the box Peter found his father's wallet, driver's license, a W-2 tax slip, a 1943 Selective Service card, his wedding ring, and his wire-rimmed glasses.

"I still have these few items in a wooden box at home, and I am thankful to have some small tokens of remembrance. But mostly, if I stop to think about it, I feel cheated and sad, like I deserved to have more of him."[25]

The end result of the search for truth was "I also understood then, with a kind of wistfulness, that, irrevocably, my life, my choices, and the person that I had become were all inseparable from the fact that my father had died."[26]

Selwyn reflects on this new reality, "This process of coming to terms with my past was not easy, but I am convinced that it saved my life, or that at the very least it enabled me to give up a burden that I had carried for almost 35 years without ever having been aware of its presence."[27]

Somewhere, as you read this book, another person like Peter—female or male—is being served up an edited version of a parent's death. Another Peter is beginning to question or launching the search for more details or is pondering a particular clue.

Sooner or later death intersects every child's life. And sooner or later the truth about the death intersects a grieving child's life. Katherine Ashenburg opens her book, *The Mourner's Dance: What We Do When People Die:* "Like many Westerners at the turn of the twenty-first century, my family and I had not much to do with death. In their twenties, my daughters had four living grandparents. Hannah had been to only two funerals in her life."[28]

Then Hannah's fianceé was in a car accident and died soon after. Hannah had only a prior limited apprenticeship with grief and ritual and now she became, in her mother's terms, "an intelligent stranger" to the reality.

Grief brings confusion, particularly the unexpected death or the traumatic death. Caroline Kennedy, for example, upon her father's death, was technically no longer part of the First Family. A new First Family took over the White House. In the midst of great grief, a grieving widow had to move immediately. But where? Other First Families have months to transition; Mrs. Kennedy and the children had days. In fact, the night of the assassination, there were conflicting signals about where the children should stay because of security issues. Initially, Caroline and John were driven to their maternal grandmother's. Then, at bedtime, they were taken in their pajamas back to the security of the White House.[29]

Initially, Mrs. Kennedy moved into the home of Ambassador Averill Harriman in Georgetown. Then she and the children moved to a home Mrs. Kennedy purchased in Georgetown in which designer Billy Baldwin re-created, down to the tiniest details, the White House bedrooms. Caroline gasped, "Look, everything is just like it was." But the first floor layout and the closeness to the streets allowed tourists to camp near the front door. The grieving family had little privacy. Soon, Mrs. Kennedy ordered that the drapes be kept shut.

Caroline had to face a string of secondary losses. Mrs.

Kennedy found the attention focused on the children upsetting. "The world is pouring terrible adoration at their feet and I fear for them. How can I bring them up normally?"[30]

Immediately following a death there can be a Transition Plan A and Plan B (or Z). Helping the child navigate and interpret—let alone survive the changes—is critical. Sometimes as a result of a parent's death a child must move, leaving friends, school, church, favorite restaurants, and play places. In short, he or she leaves the world of familiar. That's why it is important that as a compassionate care-er, decision makers are urged to consider the impact of decisions on the child. You've heard the question: "Yes, but is it good for the child?" I would ask, "Is it good for *this* grieving child at *this* moment?"

For some families, keeping the home is out of the question in light of new financial realities. It often takes two incomes to keep the wolf from the door. Many families are stunned by the immediate funeral and burial costs. Sometimes survivors have to go back to work long before they are ready because they're only given three to five days off following the death of an immediate family member.

The caring adult must help the child absorb this loss into an elemental understanding of death in general. Many children probably will not know another child who has lost a parent or sibling. That is why support groups are critical for the child. In the presence of other children who have lost a parent or sibling, the child will not feel as alone.

You cannot solve all of the transitional issues, but you can be there for support.

PART II

ASK: How do I help *this* child?

"Each child must be treated as a unique individual in need of compassion and support during a trying time" (William C. Kroen).[1]

Grief assaults a child's innocence. It is the responsibility of adults—and not just family members—to create a safe environment in which a child can grieve and be comforted. It is right that we ponder Isaiah's words, "The Spirit of the Sovereign LORD is on me, because the LORD has anointed me to preach good news to the poor . . . to comfort *all* who mourn, and provide for those who grieve in Zion" (61:1-3, emphasis added).

Jesus' words, "Blessed are those who mourn, for they will be comforted" (Matt. 5:4), can be translated, "Blessed are *the children* who mourn, for they *must* be comforted." The Beatitudes came from a compassionate, interruptible Master who stopped a funeral procession in order to give the deceased son back to the grief-stricken mother.

You have a chance to frame and ponder a question that may not, initially, be easily answered: Given what has happened, how do I help the children? How do I help *this* child? Following one death, it meant me watching *VeggieTales* with two young children and building castles out of building blocks that the grandson of the deceased instantly "demolished" with a plastic bowling ball. I lost track of how many times I rebuilt the castle. Later, it was listening to a child's questions at the cemetery about why an adjoining grave had a dolphin as a marker. It meant not immediately dismissing the child's conclusion, "I bet there's a dolphin buried there!" (I chose not to point out that this was unlikely since we were in West Lafayette, Indiana.)

Some children need lots of attention; some children need space. And time. And ears. And eyes. And hearts.

Ask yourself what you can do to help *this* child. As you will see in some of the stories of child-grievers in this book, some individuals have made significant differences in a grieving child's life. Others could have if they had stepped up to the plate or if they had been willing to be inconvenienced. While you cannot take away the source of the grief, you can find creative and compassionate ways to accompany the child in the grief.

In this hyperimpatient culture, remember that grief is an ongoing process. If you want to help a child, forget about the five stages of grief and the pressure to "get over it" and "move on."

[Name], I know it has been hard on you following [name's] death. I really want to help you. Can you think of some ways that I could help you?

AFFIRM this child

"But no one talked about it much; the 1950s were a time when a death or any other tragedy in a family was viewed as just that: personal. I didn't know that of course. I was only seven" (George W. Bush).[1]

Grief can be a confusing experience to children, especially when their lives are turned upside down following an unexpected death. Other survivors may be too devastated to play with or listen to or comfort this child. Grief is like an invading army occupying the home.

Early in grief children begin to wonder, even ask, "Hey, what about me?" Too often, children are on the sidelines—the secondary grievers—overlooked or sometimes excluded from attending rituals. Their grief may be disenfranchised by the statement, "Oh, children are so resilient" or "She's too young to understand." Many adults collude to keep the impact of reality from a child. Lady Bird Taylor Johnson's two brothers, away at boarding school, did not learn of their mother's death for almost a year. Their father's decision to keep the news from them, perhaps well-meaning, led to a lifelong estrangement between one son and his father.[2]

A child may be significantly impacted if the parent emotionally closest to the child or the nurturer-parent dies. The other parent—or in the case of divorce, a surviving noncustodial parent—has to figure out how to be father *and* mother or mother *and* father. The child now has to figure out how to interact with this grieving parent without the negotiating influence of the deceased parent. Relationships with grandparents and other family members on the deceased's side of the family can change or become estranged. In the case of divorced parents, the child may now have to go live with the noncustodial parent who is sometimes a parent the child barely knows.

It is important to remind the child that he or she had nothing to do with the death. In a world of unexplainable, children create explanations that can be emotionally destructive.

One of the great affirmations is to say—if it is true—"Your father/grandfather/mother/aunt really loved you. He or she thought you were a great kid. He or she was so proud of you. And you know what? Lots of people love you."

One of the best affirmations for a child is that life goes on. There will still be ball games and pizza, trips to the swimming pool and ice cream cones, the zoo and popcorn.

You can affirm the child's childhood. Find ways to tell and retell the child, "You need to keep on being a kid."

"[Name], sometimes being a kid is hard, and it's really tough when someone we love dies. Lots of children have lost a parent [or sibling, etc.] and had a lot of responsibility placed on them. I believe in you and God believes in you. How many other people can you think of that love you?"

AVOID overloading the child with too many details

"Being aware of your children's changing comprehension of death will prepare you to supply additional information as the need arises. Exposing your children to death is much like teaching them about sex. The completeness of the answer you give to those 'but how does the baby get in there?' questions increases as the need-to-know grows. And so with death" (Maureen Rank).[1]

"Why?" and "What happened?" are two tough questions children have to confront. "What now?" will be a key question for other children. In some cases, it's harder on a child since adults rely on reasoning skills to look beyond the answers and to draw conclusions.

For some, the statement, "Her body just stopped working and now she has a new body in heaven" may be sufficient as a beginning explanation. Other siblings may want more details of what the term "heart attack" means. The child may want to know if he or she or you could have a heart attack and die.

Some children will have a family member die as a result of severe trauma or suicide or murder or an act of terrorism. How do you explain to a child that a body cannot be recovered after the attack on the World Trade Center? How can we expect a child to comprehend such a nightmare?

After an air crash, the Federal Aviation Authority issues preliminary findings on the cause; months or years later, there will be a fuller explanation. That's wise guidance for adults explaining death. Now may be a time for an "initial" conversation of explanation. However, in the future, disclosure may have to be revisited and enhanced according to the child's comprehension skills.

You must take into consideration that a child will hear—or overhear—details or interpretations that may confuse or even undermine the child's trust. It is important to leave the door open to future conversations and clarifications. "You know, if you ever hear something that confuses you, come and talk to me. Sometimes even adults get details mixed up."

Weigh this child's need to know.

[Name], I realize that it must be very hard for you to understand death. Sometimes it's hard for adults to understand death too. I want you to feel you can come to me with questions. I will do my best to find answers for them.

ASSESS: To whom is this child listening?

"Your child may be exposed to unthinking comments by relatives and friends which only create new anxieties" (Helen Fitzgerald).[1]

In some families there are individuals who take it upon themselves to "get the facts out." Sometimes, the truth—or an interpretation of it—can be let out of the bag accidentally. Nevertheless, the damage is still done.

In one family an 18-year-old son committed suicide. Although the father and mother accepted the death as a suicide, the grandmother of the young man rejected that conclusion. "I had just talked to him. He had everything to live for! I think it was an accident." Now the 9-year-old sibling is caught between the two opinions in the family. Who should be believed: parent or grandparent?

It is one thing that an individual dies. How or why an individual dies can be troubling.

You may remember the chorus, "Oh, be careful little mouth what you say . . ." for while "the Father up above is looking down in love" there may be a child taking in more than you desire. What Sister Joanne Frey observed of six-year-old Caroline Kennedy is true for other children, "After her father died, she picked up on everything that was going on around her."[2] Caplan adds, "Lacking the capacity for adult discrimination" in sorting language and meaning, "children absorb impressions like a sponge."[3]

Phyllis Silverman, after a distinguished career working with grieving children, observed,

> To understand the place of death in children's lives we need to look at the beliefs and behavior of the adults around them, as well as those of the larger society. Although death is a biological fact, what it means to us and what we teach children about it are the results of socially shaped ideas and assumptions.[4]

Individuals with strong religious opinions—and little hesitancy in sharing those views—sometimes come into the information mix. Meredith found her daughter crying one night.

"Sweetheart, what's wrong?"

"Daddy said Uncle Tommy went to hell."

"What?"

"Daddy said Uncle Tommy went to hell because he was bad."

Meredith's brother, Tom, had died of complications of AIDS. The family did not talk about the fact that Tom was gay. The child's father's interpretation of 1 Cor. 6:9-10 left no room for grace for his brother-in-law. Needless to say, it was hard for a seven-year-old who was very faith precocious to figure out who was right on the issue.

Anticipate who will talk to the child and remember, silence or discomfort also communicate to children.

In fact, because you are a trusted person in a child's life, he or she may come to you with questions before approaching a grieving parent or family member. Alan Wolfelt insists, "Grieving kids will only feel free to ask these questions of adults whom they trust."[5] When you are invited into the grieving child's world, be a good steward of that confidence. On the other hand, you may be someone the child goes to for a second opinion. Therefore, it is important to know what the parents or grandparents are saying or wish said to the child.

[Name], tell me what your parent(s) said about [name of loved one]. What have others told you? Is anything you've been told confusing you or bothering you?

ADVOCATE for this child and for grieving children

"Recognizing grief means advocating for children, affirming their value, needs, and rights as children of God who experience loss and need to grieve. It means we have to take the risk and deal with dying and what death means to us in our own lives. We need to affirm death as part of life, not the enemy of it. We need to be people who are willing to see a different sense of life that comes to us, even in death" (Dick Gilbert).[1]

"This child may not be able to ask for what he or she needs or even know what he or she needs. A caring adult becomes involved in the child's life and opens doors for the recognition of the needs of the child. Think of the adults in this child's life. How many are grief-friendly? How many are offering clichés, the child's equivalent of pats on the head? How many are clarifying and reassuring the child that his or her fears will be taken seriously?"[2]

Linda Goldman insists that we communicate to the school system "and other caring individuals that this is a grieving child."[3]

For example, you might talk to the Sunday School teacher or public school teacher. You are not interfering; you are lobbying. This might be the first time a teacher has had a pupil in grief, and that teacher may feel overwhelmed.

Remember, by helping a responsible adult with this child, you will be helping other children in the future.

[Name], is there anyone you'd like me to talk to about [name's] death? Sometimes adults do not understand what it is like for you now. I would be happy to talk to anyone on your behalf because I believe in you.

ANTICIPATE tough special days on the child's calendar

"Young children, of course, have great expectations at Christmas, and they need to know that life continues, even after the death of a loved one" (Helen Fitzgerald).[1]

Christmas, like any special day on the calendar, can be a tough time for a grieving child. In some families, the *first* Christmas after a significant death in the family will be difficult. However, the second or subsequent years can be more difficult because support has dwindled.

There are other emotionally tough or demanding days for grieving children: graduation, a soccer tournament, a play at school, a piano recital, the VBS demonstration program, or church Christmas play. I have long been moved by the story of one child on graduation night less than eight months after her father died in the collapse of the World Trade Center. None of the happy smiling "graduate and father" photo ops for this young girl on her special night. Then, just before the procession started, in walked three uniformed firefighters from her father's firehouse. No, they were not her father—but through their presence they made a tough night just a little better.

A child will often drop hints about special events coming up—a play, a party, or a science fair. Spending some time with a child or carving out time to be with the child in a particular parent's or grandparent's absence could be important.

[Name], I was so proud of you. You know, your [relationship/ name] would have been so proud of you. I am glad I got to come and see you in [this play, this band recital, etc.].

ANSWER honestly and accurately

"Kids don't ask the kinds of questions that anyone can actually answer" (Sandi Kahn Shelton).[1]

"Having answers is not nearly as important as being willing to deal with the questions" (Kathyrn N. Chapman).[2]

Children have questions. Linda Goldman, who has worked with many grieving children, identifies the most common questions you can expect to be asked:

> What does it mean to die?
> Will I die?
> Will you die?
> Will I die in my sleep?
> Will I die if I get sick?
> Who will take care of me if you die?
> Can wishes cause death?[3]

Many children do not have sufficient vocabulary or comprehension skills to capture their questions or their fears. Victoria Alexander, whose father died by suicide when she was an adolescent, believes that grievers have three needs: to find words for the loss; to say the words out loud; and to know the words have been heard.[4]

Some individuals dodge a child's questions or give answers that are inaccurate or false. While children may not initially be able to dissect the inaccuracy of an answer, they sense the discomfort and the hesitancy in answering the question. They may not follow up with a "Then how come . . ." question, but they can sense the inadequacy of the answer. Kathyrn Chapman reminds would-be helpers:

> To be significant adults who give children what they need, expect, and deserve calls forth our very best. We can't find all the necessary knowledge from books, though they do enlighten us. We can't collect a bag of tricks, though know-how is important. What matters is the kind of person we are. We must, therefore, take responsibility for nurturing

ourselves and all the relationships that feed our selfhood, including our relationship to God. We nourish children from overflow, not from emptiness.[5]

If you mislead a child with half-truths or falsehoods, he or she may not bring future questions to you or trust your answers or trust the answers of another adult. Remember, "Family secrets don't last long in most families."[6]

Not only should a child's questions be answered in a straightforward, direct fashion, but noted bereavement specialist Robert Neimeyer insists that answers must take into some consideration, "the family's shared beliefs regarding family roles, separation, death or the afterlife." Given the religious diversity in families today, there is a wide network of shared beliefs. Still Neimeyer contends, "If children are old enough to formulate questions about these losses, they are old enough to deserve appropriate answers."[7]

Child psychologist Linda Goldman calms the anxiety when she reminds us, "It's OK that we don't know the answers."[8]

[Name], tell me what your family has told you about that question.

ATTEND rituals

"Going to someone's funeral or memorial service is one way to let a family [and a child] know you share some of their sadness . . . and some of their good memories, too" (Laurie Krasny Brown and Marc Brown).[1]

One gift you can give a child is to attend ritual(s) for the child's loved one even if you did not know the deceased. A familiar face can be a significant comfort to a child. If you do not know the family, briefly introduce yourself to some adult family members and explain your relationship to the child.

Pray before you go and pray before you enter the church or funeral home. Pray in your heart for individuals who appear to be distressed, even if you do not know their names—God does. Pray for this child.

Sign the guest book because, in their distress, family members may forget your name.

Some families may be too overwrought to adequately recognize or remember your attendance. Your name in the book will help remind them.

[Name], I wanted to come here so that I could tell you how sorry I am that your [name/relationship] died. This is probably very hard for you to understand. I am going to be praying that Jesus will make you feel very loved. And one thing that helps me is to know that I can talk to God anytime.

AVOID euphemisms

"Ask your child if she is hearing any words she doesn't understand" (Helen Fitzgerald).[1]

Trying to explain death can be challenging. If adults who have some level of vocabulary development and comprehension of death rely on clichés and euphemisms to communicate about death, it is even more so for children. Children overhear euphemisms that can be bewildering.

Clichés are a shorthand effort to talk about death without talking about death.

So, a child hears:

"She's in a better place . . ."

"The Lord took him . . ."

"He's asleep . . ."

One child heard, "God needed another singer in the choir" as an explanation for her sibling's death. So, to avoid being the next singer in God's choir, she stopped singing. In her reasoning, if she did not sing very well, God would not want her in His choir.

Remember, a child's reasoning does not have to make sense to an adult.

[Name], if I ever use any words that confuse you, I want you to tell me. And if I am not available, who could you ask?

BE there for the child!

"Some adults may assume that children do not have the same need as an adult to grieve the loss of others. In situations of crisis and loss, children are sometimes pushed aside or protected from the pain. They can feel afraid, abandoned, and lonely . . . experiencing a loss in childhood can have serious effects later in life" *(Fundamentals of Nursing)*.[1]

One gift an adult can give a child is his or her presence in the child's life. Many children relish time more than stuff, so make time for this child. Remember, the time spent with a grieving child will bless you as well.

Christopher Andersen, in *The Day John Died*, described an incident that took place in January 1964 as Sister Joanne Frey taught a catechism class about Mary Magdalene bathing Jesus' feet. Caroline Kennedy interrupted, "My mommy cries all the time." The nun tried to overlook the six-year-old to return the focus to the lesson. Caroline interrupted insistently, "My mommy cries *all the time.*" As the determined nun again tried to return the attention of the class to Mary Magdalene and Jesus, Caroline loudly said: "After my daddy died, my mommy is always crying. I go and get in bed with her and tell her everything is all right and tell her to stop crying. But she doesn't. My mommy is always crying. . . ."[2]

At that moment the wise teacher abandoned the curriculum and asked Caroline to come sit on her lap. It was a moment for comforting a child. Years later, Sister Joanne noted, "She just had to tell somebody what was happening behind closed doors. It was a cry for help. Obviously the poor little girl didn't know what to do."[3]

This child you are comforting has "closed doors" too. Listen for that faint cry for help.

Dietrich Bonhoeffer insisted in his classic *Life Together*, "We must be ready to allow ourselves to be interrupted by God. God will be constantly crossing our paths and cancelling our plans by sending us people with claims and petitions."[4] Some of those people are children. If Jesus could be interrupted by children, so can you! I do not think this adaptation does violence to Scripture, "Let the little [grieving] children come to me, and do not hinder them" (Luke 18:16). Take a moment and think about the ways adults hinder children.

Too many individuals spend time trying to determine what to do *for* a child. Make some time to be *with* this child.

[Name], I will do my best to be here for you. Sometimes I may not understand or you may have to remember to tell me something later. But you will always be on my mind.

BE real!

"We cannot protect children from knowing death and from mourning by diverting their attention" (Phyllis Silverman).[1]

We can support children as they experience mourning by being real and not trying to sugarcoat death. I have wondered what it must have been like at young John Kennedy's third birthday party just hours after his father was buried at Arlington as the president's brokenhearted brothers and presidential aides ate cake and watched the child open presents. To their credit, they showed up.

Children who are grieving may be wiser than their chronological age. Some adults try to offer a religious-soaked, syrupy "It will all be better soon" approach. Children may have a keener sense of reality or a suspicion that those words are merely a cliché that comforts the adult.

Choose your words carefully. A piece of Amish wisdom will help you: "Listen much, talk little."

[Name], I am going to try out how to talk to you without talking down to you. There is a lot about [name's] death that I do not understand. So, sometime you may have to remind me that you are a child. If I am not making sense, will you tell me?

CELEBRATE heaven

"My Grandma is in Heaven and I wish I could visit her for a holiday, because when she went away she didn't say good-bye" (Dean).[1]

Ethel Young describes her 11-year-old grandson Andrew's curiosity about heaven after the death of his grandfather, her husband, Harold, whom the grandchildren called Buppy.

"Gramma, is heaven real or is it just a fairy tale?"

Not having enough faith of her own to answer that question, Ethel replied, "Well, Buppy thought heaven was a real place because he said this world is not fair, and he believed there had to be a place where everything was fair." Ethel and Andrew then talked about the unfairness of children who suffer. "Buppy believed there was a place where the crooked was made straight and the rough places were made smooth. That's heaven, Andrew."

Ethel concludes, "And that satisfied him."[2] Sometimes children borrow theological ideas from significant adults in their lives or, in a multicultural society, from other children—sometimes from children who follow other world religions. As one child told Timothy Freke, "In Heaven you can either go back to earth to put right your wrongs or stay in heaven."[3] That sounds more like reincarnation than orthodox Christianity, but it may be a significant comfort to a child whose father was abusive.

Some adults in a grieving child's life do not believe in heaven or eternal life. You may have to balance your words with the beliefs of a parent or guardian. Elizabeth Reed suggests, "If a parent does not believe in a future life, he can help his child best by being humbly honest with him and, at the same time, see to it that he has the opportunity to learn about the faith of those who do believe. Thus, the door will be open to him to search and find his own faith."[4]

On the other hand, adults have an opportunity to learn about heaven from the perspective of children. A 10-year-old whose mother and younger brother had been killed in an automobile accident was admitted to Louisville Children's Hospital. Because she had some questions about heaven, Chaplain Ronald Oliver went to talk with her. Specifically, she wanted to know if her mother and brother were OK in heaven.

She followed up with questions about heaven. "What is it like?" "What are they doing?" "Are they OK?" Chaplain Oliver asked about her religious background.

"Has anyone ever talked with you about heaven?"

"We had a dog die one time. My mother said she went to heaven."

"Did your mom tell you what heaven was like?"

"Yes." Mom said, "'Heaven is the place where nothing ever goes wrong.'"

Before replying, Oliver pondered his words.

There was only one thing to say, "Your mom is exactly right. Heaven is a place where nothing ever goes wrong."

Chaplain and patient continued to talk, wondering what her mother and brother were doing at that moment in heaven. "We wondered what it was like to meet their dog. We agreed that it is OK to be sad even if Mom and Brother are OK and happy. They will be missed."[5]

How would you have answered this child's question?

There is no age qualification on Jesus' words, "Do not let your hearts be troubled. . . . I am going there to prepare a place for you" (John 14:1, 2). In fact, in many ways, heaven may be easier for children to believe.

One morning my friend Nancy happened to tell her seven-year-old Elliott that "today would have been your grandmother's birthday."

"Can we still have a birthday cake?"

"Sure," Nancy agreed. Moments later Elliott asked. "But how will Grandma get her slice of cake up in heaven?" Then he answered his own question, "I know. We can send it up on a spaceship." Nancy explained that the cake would be stale by the time they could get it there but that his grandmother would appreciate his thoughtfulness.

That night as the family gathered around the birthday cake,

Elliott announced, "We have to sing happy birthday so loud that Grandma will hear it all the way up in heaven." And they did.

Sadly, not all adults in a child's life may believe in heaven and may, for whatever reason, share their perspective with the grieving child and take away or diminish the child's hope.

You may want to take a moment to share John 14:2 with the child. "In my Father's house are many rooms . . . I am going there to prepare a place for *you*." Help the child locate this promise in his or her Bible.

Caroline Kennedy had questions about heaven. Through tears she asked Maude Shaw, "But what will Daddy do in heaven?"

"I am sure God is giving him enough things to do, because he was always such a busy man. God has made your daddy a guardian angel for you and for Mommy and for John."[6] (Two-day-old Patrick Kennedy had died on August 9, 1963. Thus Caroline had lost a brother and a father within 90 days.)

Alan Wolfelt encourages adults, "Be his sounding board about this important issue. If he has doubts or fears, help him express them."[7] This might be a good time to have a child draw a picture of heaven.

[Name], has anyone ever asked you to come over to his or her house and play? Well, I think sometimes God says, "Can you come to My house called heaven?" And we miss our loved one a lot, but we remind ourselves that someday everyone we love who loves Jesus will join us for a special party. Matter of fact, I think that every day in heaven is a party. And it's OK to be sad even when we know [name] is in heaven.

CHILD-SIZE the holidays

"Holidays can be particularly stressful to kids. Although children often delight in family gatherings and can extract the essence of them in ways that adults may have lost, stress remains. Kids have their own anxieties about many things that adults often fail to appreciate. They may be anxious simply in terms of getting the gifts they want, or more significantly in negotiating their way through the masses of known and unknown family and friends, foods and environments" (Mariana Caplan).[1]

Christmas presents a significant challenge for the grieving child. Norman Rockwell never drew the *grieving* family in a Christmas setting. Some grieving families scale back Christmas plans and focus on the children. Some families, unfortunately, skip Christmas or any special holiday. Some mothers—once the Christmas magicians who made everything magical—may be incapable of even the simplest decorating. Or it may be the mom who died.

In some families, the loss of a second income or the funeral costs may mean Christmas significantly different from previous holidays.

Help the child find ways to symbolize the loss of a parent, family member, or friend through creating a special ornament or poem or piece of artwork. Buy a clear plastic ornament and ask the child to put something inside or insert a small picture.

Remember that a grieving child may become frustrated when he or she overhears all the holiday excitement other children are experiencing.

[Name], is there a way you would like to celebrate this Christmas? Is there something I can do to help you to get ready for Christmas? (Example: Going with the child to the mall to pick out a Christmas gift for the surviving parent or to child-sit with this child while the parent goes shopping.)

CREATE a collage

"Ask the child how he or she wants to remember his or her loved one who has died and then help the child find ways to do this" (Theresa Huntley).[1]

You've heard that a picture is worth a thousand words. Pictures help grievers remember. Unfortunately, some think that the goal of grief is to forget the loved one or to get over a loved one. No. The goal is to remember. Parenthetically, this can become a significant issue if the surviving parent moves to remarry immediately and intends to "replace" the missing parent.

Collages are an effective way children can organize their memories. A collage is a story—the story of the relationship between the deceased and the collage-maker. Through selecting pictures, words, and images from magazines a child can "make a story" and create memory.

Take a sheet of poster paper (36" x 24"). Tell the child the goal is to "capture" the loved one by cutting pictures or words from the magazines. Have the child look through magazines and find pictures that tell the stories of the loved one and/or the relationship. After the child has a number of pictures or words, ask him or her to arrange, trim, and paste them onto the poster paper with a glue stick. (Some children may want to try them out in different spaces before pasting them on.) Note: Do not get obsessed with neatness. Do not edit the child's choices as inappropriate. A collage is for the child's benefit.

[Name], this is a creative experience. Suppose you had to tell about [name of your loved one] to a complete stranger. What pictures would you use?

Let the child have the freedom to do the collage in his or her own way. There is no right or wrong way for a child to create a collage. Some of the best collages are a bit messy or over-done. Let the child be creative. If the child doesn't see some words or phrases, use magic markers or colored pens.

Ask the child to tell you about the pictures he or she chose. Explain to the child that he or she can add pictures to the collage from time to time, or the child may have photographs he or she wishes to include.

Commend the child on the finished collage.

For 10 years in a hospital setting I have worked with griev-ers making collages. This is a way to tell a story. It has been for some an incredible way to "corral" words and memories in or-der to tell the story of a deceased loved one.

[Name], you have done such a great job with your collage. Tell me about this picture. Why did you place it here?

COMMEMORATE the life

"The life of every person who dies need to be commemorated if we are to teach children that all lives have value" (Sandra Fox).[1]

There may be some temptation to elevate the deceased to sainthood in the immediacy of the death. In some cases, the deceased, if a sibling, becomes the standard for the child to measure up to. In other cases, the child's grief becomes complicated because he or she cannot acknowledge pain the deceased caused him or her. Eventually, the adult child will have to deal with the issue.

In Judaism, there is a guiding principle of *hesped*—or balanced, truthful eulogy. Children and adults have to "own" the real individual, not a carefully cleaned-up version.

As a child I was terrorized by a music supervisor who periodically swept into our elementary classroom and "terrorized" the students—and as I later discovered—some teachers. She would demand that the students sing a particular song and would walk row-by-row listening to individuals. I have blocked from my memory my first experience with Miss Helen. I was deeply apprehensive about a forthcoming visit. An appearance by Miss Helen in her all-black outfits could be the talk of the playground and the bus ride home. Fearing a visit, over dinner one night I moaned what I and a playmate moaned on the playground, "I wish she would die."

Early one morning my mother walked into my bedroom and awakened me, "Well, you got your wish. Miss Helen McBride is dead!" Imagine the weight on my six-year-old heart: I was responsible for her death. I went to school with great fear and trepidation. What if my teacher put two-and-two together? What if my principal found out? Maybe they already knew. Would the police be waiting to arrest me?

I know now that I was not responsible. But I also know that the woman terrorized me. Ironically, at the first PTA meeting after her death, our class sang a song to honor her service in the Jefferson County Public Schools. I did not sing loudly that night.

Children may need help balancing the eulogy with the good and the bad. They may need you to alleviate their confusion.

Help the child create something cherishable.

Gene Shrader, our principal, helped me deal with Miss Helen's death. After we sang our special in her honor, he told the entire gathering of students and parents, "I know Miss Helen terrorized me as a child . . . and she *still* terrorized me as a principal."

[Name], sometimes life is like a seesaw. When one child weighs too much, the seesaw is tilted. But if you work at it, you can balance the seesaw. Sometimes, a person did things that are hard to forget because it hurt us or hurt our feelings. Can you think of the worst thing [name] did to you? (Give the child time.) Now, can you think of something nice [name] did for you?

DE-FAULT the child

"This is the time, too, to assure your children that the baby's death is not their fault. If your children are older, they may have resented the idea of a new baby invading their territory. And they need a clear reassurance that vacillating feelings about a new baby are very normal and that they in no way affected the outcome of the pregnancy" (Maureen Rank).[1]

During their years of "magical thinking" when children presume responsibility far beyond reality, a death can prompt an undue sense of responsibility that can last well into adulthood. One 49-year-old wrote Dear Abby about an ugly encounter between her and her father. The girl did something and then stormed out of the room to the basement. Her angry father followed her and said, "Your mother is upstairs dying by inches, and you're mostly responsible for it!"

This child had no idea that her mother was dying. Years later, after extensive counseling over the incident "and how the situation was handled," she still feels robbed and abandoned.[2]

Remember, some children will *create* explanations rather than live in the absence of an explanation. For one young girl, the brutal reality that her mother had died was too difficult to endure. Denied the opportunity of attending her mother's funeral, "For a long time," Rosie O'Donnell would later explain, "I didn't believe it." So, she created the fantasy that her mother, "perhaps, tired of bringing up five children, had run off to California, but one day would certainly return."[3]

Be cautious in how you receive and discount the child's assumed responsibility. Weeks after a bombing tragedy at a school in Houston in which a principal, two children, and a deranged man were killed and numerous students were injured, Susan Cooley, a classmate and good friend of one of the boys who died, came to her mother to tell her that she had "killed the principal" and children. Her mother, knowing the details of the incident, wondered how the child could possibly believe that.

Susan said that when the recess bell had rung she had not run outside but had gone to the bathroom. When she flushed the toilet, the most dreadful noise happened and all the windows blew out. Therefore she had killed her classmate and the principal.

Barbara Bush, who included the story in her memoirs, noted, "This sounds slightly crazy, but that's what this little girl thought."[4] The story emphasizes that children need to be not only seen in times of tragedy but also heard. What if this child had labored on under this heavy load of assumed guilt?

"[Name], sometimes kids think they are responsible for some-one's death. Nothing you said or thought caused [name's] death. You are not to blame!

DRAW and COLOR

"Drawing gives them a way to let their feelings flow onto paper. When no one tells them how or what to draw, drawing becomes cathartic. Children should be free to choose whether to share and discuss their drawings with others or to keep them private" (William C. Kroen).[1]

If you want to know what's going on in a grieving child's mind, give the child paper and crayons or markers.

Initially, you might bring some new crayons and markers and an artist's sketch pad to the child at the funeral home. Suggest, "I thought you might like to draw some pictures with me that you could put in the casket." Or "Pictures that would help you remember this experience." Increasingly, many child-friendly funeral homes have art supplies to resource a child's grief during a visitation or funeral.

The drawings could be a child's gift to the deceased, to display at the visitation or on a memory table, to give to a particular griever, or to keep.

Draw or color with the child rather than observe. Fern Reiss advises, "Don't make suggestions, just draw. Let your child lead, and you follow."[2] Most children are more than willing to share their crayons. Something you draw might ignite the child's curiosity or creativity or jump-start a memory or conversation. To level the playing field, draw or color with your nondominant hand.

Ask the child to talk about the picture. One friend asked a child in a single-parent family to draw a picture of something he and his family loved to do. The child drew a beach scene. As my friend looked at the drawing she noticed an extra figure in the "day at the beach" drawing. She asked, "Who is this?" pointing to the mother, sister, little brother. Finally, she pointed to the figure stretched out on a beach towel in a Speedo swimsuit. "And who is this?"

"Oh, that's God. He always goes along with us to the beach.

That way if my mom dozes off, God will be there to keep an eye on us."

The photo captured a theological principle embedded in this grieving child's mind. If God is with us in the "valley of the shadow of death," why wouldn't God be with a grieving family on an outing to the beach?

Drawings give adults a chance to launch meaningful conversations with children and to learn from a child's perspective of the loss. William Worden offers these suggestions for the child:

- Draw something you worry about.
- Draw something that makes you mad.
- Draw yourself and write words that describe you.
- Draw your favorite memory of your dead father, mother, sister, etc.
- Draw a recent dream that you have had.
- Draw the ugliest picture that you can.
- Draw your family.
- Draw yourself before your loved one died; draw yourself now.
- Draw something that scares you.
- Draw a picture of heaven.[3]

If the child gives you the picture, consider it an important gift.

[Name], some kids try to hide their feelings. But I think that it is important to acknowledge our feelings. Sometimes, we cannot change our sadness, but we can share it with someone. Anytime you want to share a picture with me, I would be happy to see it."

DO NOT DISTRACT this child from grief

"Children seem to have a sixth sense about any disruption in the emotional tenor of their home. When you're under pressure, they feel it. That is why it is important to keep communicating, so that they know this time of sadness was not caused by them, and that it will be over" (Maureen Rank).[1]

I'd be rich if I had a dollar for each time someone told a griever, "Stay busy!" Many adults operate with a frantic, "Keep 'em occupied." This definitely doesn't work with children. Some children are already too busy with soccer, dance classes, piano lessons, tennis, church activities, and so forth. In fact, it can be difficult if the child loses his or her "chauffeur" who co-ordinates the activities and gets the child there. Some children have to drop out of important activities or activities that would have been helpful in the transition to the new reality because they cannot get to an activity or cannot afford it.

I concede that the old Appalachian folk tune, "You've got to walk that lonesome valley . . . you've got to walk it by yourself" primarily applies to adults. Yet, as I ponder it, this is a reality for children too. They do have to walk a "valley" that other children with intact families don't.

Trips or excursions to Toys-R-Us, in the long run, are not going to be helpful if the goal is to hold at bay the reality of wrestling with grief.

[Name], when something like [name's] death happens, it's hard to understand. Does your teacher ever say: "[Child's name], pay attention!" Well, we have to pay attention to grief even though it hurts. But, you know what? Grief is like a hard teacher at school. We learn a lot, and what we learn will help other kids who are grieving.

ENCOURAGE keeping routines

"Being patient doesn't mean allowing inappropriate behavior. Children need limits, especially when their emotions are in turmoil and their lives have been turned upside down by a loved one's death . . . Be clear with your children about what you expect from them" (William C. Kroen).[1]

It's reality that some grieving children learn how to manipulate adults. This may begin when the child is allowed to stay up late when the child protests being afraid to go to bed or to sleep alone or is afforded other previously denied privileges.

It is tempting as a coach or teacher or friend to grant special favors to the grieving child—favors that other children will recognize and resent. Be sure you have a good reason for choices you make.

Maintaining pregrief routines offers structure to children—structure that may be especially beneficial for a grieving child.

[Name], sometimes when we're grieving, we don't feel like doing things like cleaning our rooms or doing schoolwork. But routines really help us because they give us something to focus on. A routine is a way of keeping us going. Is there something you are having a hard time doing?

FINANCE counseling

"I do not feel she has much chance, poor soul" (Edith Roosevelt).[1]

"The longest established local hospices are usually the best facilities to attain a referral for an excellent grief therapist. Physicians tend to refer to psychiatrists and very few psychiatrists have been trained in grief and bereavement. Hospice staffs, who are actively engaged in assisting bereaved families, usually have a full awareness of the various services and grief therapists available in their community" (James A. Fogarty).[2]

No one thought the eight-year-old had much of a chance, given the dysfunction of her family. The father, an alcoholic who had fathered a child with one of the family maids, was ostracized from prominent social circles. The child's parents were separated—a scandal in itself in those days—when the mother died with diphtheria. This mother, for some reason, had repeatedly berated the child for her looks. "You will have to be good because no one will ever love you for your looks." One winter day before Christmas 1892, as eight-year-old Eleanor pondered the confusion in her family, Susie Parish, an aunt, walked in and informed her, "Your mother is dead."

That death took away the child's hope of ever winning her mother's love. A menagerie of "ifs" troubled her: "If she had been jollier, more attractive, more compatible, better behaved, would her mother have lived?" Maybe her mother could in time have come to love her.[3]

"With her mother's death, she became an outsider, always expecting betrayal and abandonment . . . For the rest of her life her actions were in part an answer to her mother. If she were really good, then perhaps nobody else would leave her, and people would see the love in her heart."[4]

More loss and turmoil came when the child's young brother died 12 months later. Then, unbelievably, her father died 12 months after that. Before age 10, this child experienced three significant deaths within a 24-month period. In those days, there were no skilled professionals and organizations to support grieving children.

Despite the sanction of the family, the child idolized her father and refused to believe he was gone forever." Because her hypervigilant grandmother refused to allow her to attend her father's funeral, there was no closure provided or allowed. The powerful feelings Elliott elicited in his young daughter of powerful but ultimately tragic and flawed love would remain shut down in her heart until awakened again in another powerful relationship.[5]

Years of great emotional pain ensued until Madame Marie Souvestre, a teacher at Allenswood School in Paris, took a special interest in this adolescent, and that made a lasting difference in the girl's world—and some would argue, American history—because the girl was Eleanor Roosevelt, first lady, 1933-45.[6]

Counseling offers, in William Worden's view, five gifts to a child:

- helps facilitate the various tasks of mourning
- provides children with acceptable outlets for their feelings, including ways to address their fears and concerns
- helps children get answers to their questions
- helps counter misconceptions that children have about the death—and death in general
- makes discussions of death a normal part of the child's experience, something that may not be happening at home or in other settings.[7]

In a peer grief group, children receive support from a trained leader and from other children. Involvement in a group "gives the child the reassurance that he or she is not alone in the experience of loss."[8] This is critically important because in dozens of ways a child who has lost a parent will be reminded, sometimes cruelly by classmates, that he or she does not have a mother or father.

Are there ways you can make counseling possible? The Bureau of the Census reports that 5.7 million children are not covered by medical insurance and thus do not receive professional care.[9] You could be making an investment in a future first lady, scientist, humanitarian, diplomat, or pastor. In time, Eleanor Roosevelt grew up to write the Universal Declaration of Human Rights, serve as an ambassador to the United Nations, and become one of the most admired women in the world. You might want to share a biography of Eleanor Roosevelt with the child.

Not every child needs or will need to see a psychologist or counselor for grief-related issues. In the Child Bereavement Study, one-third of the grieving children had some emotional or behavioral problems that warranted "some type of counseling intervention during the first two years of bereavement."[10] Worden offers this guiding philosophy of intervention: "To identify early those most in need of screening and to intervene."[11]

Every child deserves solid, grief-aware helpers to help him or her navigate and, as he or she grows up, renegotiate at critical developmental moments the significant losses of life.

Money may be tight in a family that has experienced a death. The average funeral cost in the United States is $6,130 (this does not include cemetery costs and flowers).[12] On which credit card could *you* put $6,130? Imagine writing a check for $6,130. Now, imagine what a particular family may be economically facing.

Forty-three million Americans do not have medical insurance (which in some plans includes psychological services).[13] Some coverage provides only a limited number of visits with a mental health professional or does not provide coverage for visits to a skilled child bereavement specialist. Too often, grieving family members are told, "Oops. Coverage is over. You are on your own."

In rural areas there may not be mental health professionals who specialize in children or grief, and counselors who work with adults may not be effective with children.

One of the gifts you can provide a grieving child is, in essence, a "gift certificate" for counseling.

My family never sent flowers following a death. My dad explained, "That family can't eat flowers next week." The money expended on flowers could finance a significant amount of counseling care for a child.

Unfortunately, there are some strongly opinioned counseling resisters in the Christian community. Earl Grollman reminds us, "There are times when even the best informed and well-intentioned adults are simply inadequate. Getting professional assistance is not an admission of weakness but a demonstration of real love and strength."[14]

[Name], when we are sick, sometimes we go to a doctor. Sometimes that doctor sends us to see another doctor called a specialist. A counselor is a specialist who understands grief and can help you make more sense of some of the things you are thinking and feeling since [name's] death.

FUND some special events

"Do everything you can to help Zenas the lawyer and Apollos on their way and see that they have everything they need" (Titus 3:13).

Every child needs fun—otherwise you end up with an adult miser like Ebenezer Scrooge (the Dickens' character in *Christmas Carol* who lost both parents as a child—a common experience in the Dickens era). Your financial gift could help a child on his or her way to integrating the loss.

Initially, funding some special events may sound like a contradiction of the earlier point of not attempting to distract the child, but also remember that what previously was part of the child's normal life may become a luxury due to loss of an income or increased debt from burial expenses.

Attending a children's grief camp may be a wonderful experience for you to make happen for a grieving child or adolescent. Check around for grief camps for children sponsored by hospitals, hospices, churches, and other social organizations. A funeral director may be the first contact.

- Write a check to sponsor the child's participation.
- Buy extra tickets to an athletic event.
- Give a gift card to a movie theater or bookstore.

Remember to clear specific or large gifts with the surviving parent. The last thing a grieving parent needs is the equivalent of a "gift pony." In some cases, you may have to explain the significance of a particular sporting event as in "Your dad always loved the Broncos . . . or the Yankees."

In some cases, taking the child to the activity relieves the grieving parent and may establish an opportunity to talk.

[Name], some people expect kids to be sad all the time after someone they love dies. But God did not make kids to be sad all the time. Sometimes a great kid like you needs a break. It's OK to have fun. Can you remember some times you and [name] had fun? Fun is another way of creating memories.

GIVE the child permission to grieve

"People [children] need an opportunity to hurt out loud" (Lady Bird Johnson).[1]

In a culture that prizes "moving on" or "getting over it," giving permission to grieve sounds like an alien concept. However, if you have ever overheard someone tell a child, "Now you've got to help your mother" or "Be the man around the house," you know that adults can unknowingly withhold permission to grieve.

Dexter King writes about one change following the death of his father, Martin Luther King. The four King children were blessed to have many surrogate father figures like Granddaddy King, Uncle A. D. (A. D. Williams King, Martin's brother), Uncle Andy (Andrew Young), and Uncle Harry (Belafonte). Nevertheless, Coretta Scott King told Martin III, her oldest son, that he was "the head of the house now." Younger brother Dexter recalls, "Martin took it to heart," creating tensions between the three older children, "with him suddenly trying to be the man, with no model."[2]

Appendix B offers a special permission to mourn slip for children.

[Name], at your school, do you have to have a permission slip to do certain things like go on a field trip? Well, I have a very special permission slip for you. [Give the child the form.] This is a permission to grieve form. If someone tells you that "You shouldn't be grieving because . . . ," just remember this form gives you permission. You might want to put it on your wall at home or keep it in a special place.

GUARD confidences shared by a child

"We bury little Ellie tomorrow up at Tivoli by Mother's side. He is happy in Heaven with her, so now you must not grieve or sorrow" (Elliott Roosevelt to his daughter Eleanor following her brother's death) (David Roosevelt).[1]

Building trust with a grieving child can be challenging following a traumatic death or during a dysfunctional family's expression of grief. There can be so many people around that it is hard for the child to have an anchor point or full access to his or her parents or surviving parent. The child, nevertheless, needs to talk.

Confidences are a delicate line to walk. In one situation, the child was so overwhelmed by his brother's death that he concluded that he would have to abandon his own dream of an exchange semester in Europe in order to take care of his parents. As I talked to him, I suggested we wait and see. However, I eventually broke that confidence by telling the father, "You need to think about how this impacts your surviving son and how he thinks it may play out. In a sense, he is co-grieving the death of his brother *and* the death of his dream."

"Oh, no," the father responded, "of course we still want him to go."

"Then you need to communicate that to him. Soon."

In talking to a grieving child you may discover an awareness of family history and reality that does not coincide with a public image. Not every deceased individual, to a child, is a "loved one." Some families have significant secrets.

Remember also that some children have been powerless in dysfunctional family dynamics. The deceased may have been the parent the child perceived as the primary antagonist or barrier to family peace. Simply put, for some children grief brings an element of relief into their worlds. The deceased may have been abusive to the child—at least in ways the child counts as abusive. For example, they may not have gotten along well with a stepparent or with a live-in (and given the number of live-in relationships, this is a significant issue for stress on children). On the other hand, that initial sense of relief may bring guilt that needs to be confronted.

[Name], every child has things that bother him or her that are hard to understand. If there is ever anything you want to tell me that may be hard to tell others, I will listen to you. It won't be like a secret, but I promise to listen to you very carefully because you are very important. Some things are just too big for a kid to keep inside.

GO to the cemetery or scattering area

"Though he never knew any of those with whose memories we come to commune—my father, my mother, Aunt Rose, and a baby brother who died before I was born—they have made their mark on him just as surely as though he had grown up among them in that small Bronx apartment of such emotional turbulence. But none of them has affected his life more than my father" (Sherwin Nuland explaining why he takes his son to the cemetery).[1]

Some families do not go back to the cemetery after the committal; some do not allow children to attend the committal —too depressing. "He's not there! Why should we go to the cemetery?" Some adults are afraid of confusing the child or fear questions like:

"Does he still have to go to the bathroom?"

"Won't he get cold?"

"If Grandma is in heaven, why do we come here?"

Ideally, children will have been positively introduced to a cemetery before there is a personal experience with a burial. Unfortunately, too many adults scare children by saying things like, "Ohhhh, a cemetery. Betcha there are ghosts in there!" Adults may unknowingly plant ideas that eventually have to be uprooted.

Some family members may want to use a cemetery as a way to pass on family stories or traditions. Cemeteries are a way to keep connection with our dead. For centuries cemeteries were part of churches and were called graveyards. To go to church you passed the cemetery. Before the concept of "perpetual care," because families were responsible for the upkeep of the graves, families went periodically to trim or cut the grass, to rake the leaves, to tend flowers. As they worked, stories were passed on to the next generation.

A surviving parent may not want to go to the cemetery for fear of breaking down in front of the child. You might, with the parent's permission, volunteer to take the child if the child would like to visit the grave.

The great theologian Henri Nouwen wrote the family of his friend, Bob, whose wife had chosen not to allow her two young sons to attend his funeral. Thus, the cemetery—for the sons—"remained a fearful and dangerous place." One day, the widow asked Nouwen to go to the cemetery with her and the boys, although the oldest son refused. So, the three of them sat on the grave and reminisced about a "kind and gentle man" named Bob.

I said, "Maybe, one day we should have a picnic here. This is not only a place to think about death, but also a place to rejoice in life. I think Bob will be most honored when we find new strength here, to live." At first it seemed a strange idea: having a meal on top of a tombstone. But isn't that similar to what Jesus told His disciples to do when He asked them to share bread and wine in His memory?

Days later, the mother took her eldest child to the grave, her sister having convinced her that there was nothing to fear. "Now they often go to the cemetery and tell each other stories about Bob."[2] (If you decide to try a cemetery picnic, check with the cemetery office because some cemeteries have policies barring such activities.)

Check to see if there are any prominent citizens or historical personalities buried in the cemetery. This could be a way of passing on an interest in history.

Keep track of special days—such as birthdays or Easter or Christmas or Mother's Day—for a visit. Visiting the cemetery is a way of helping a child actively remember and honor his or her loved ones, as my friend Todd Little discovered when one of his triplets asked, "Can we go visit Mommy at the cemetery for Mother's Day?" He explains:

So there I was, walking through the cemetery with triplets, answering questions about life and love. There were questions about burial, cremation, and embalming, and I pointed out where their former teacher's husband rests. We admired a new monument to a well-known local attorney recently deceased. And we talked about respect for the dead and the importance of maintaining a connection—honoring those we love who are no longer with us, remembering their lives and love they gave us, and keeping them in our hearts.

None of Todd's sons was traumatized by the experience. Todd recalls, "I was struck by the beauty of these moments I shared with my sons. The time was filled with emotion and the wonder and innocence of childhood. For those moments I could almost feel the connection between the past, present and future, humanity, divinity and eternity."[3]

After leaving the cemetery, stop at a restaurant or get some ice cream as a way to "debrief." Listen to and reflect on the child's experience and share your experience. This is not a "grilling" of the child but an invitation to talk—if the child desires.

[Name], how do you remember things that are important? [After the child answers] One of the most important things we can do is to remember to remember. That is why I go to the cemetery. It is a way and a place we can remember to remember [name]. Some children do not like to go to the cemetery because it makes them sad or afraid. But other children find it a "remembering" place.

GIVE this grieving child permission to have fun

"Just like it's OK to be sad and angry, it's OK to be a kid and be happy, even if Daddy died" (Mark Scrivani).[1]

Children grieve intermittently—a reality that annoys some adults. Children still need to run and play and sing and work off excess energy. "It is not wise to neglect play," cautions Stuart Brown, founder of the Institute for Play in Carmel Valley, California.[2] Unfortunately, a death in the family has been, for some, the end of childhood.

You can help the child understand that it is OK to still be a kid—to still want to play or go somewhere like a park. Do not, however, use or encourage fun activities to distract from the grief.

[Name], your most important job is to be a kid. Some individuals may not understand why you are playing and having fun so soon after [name's] death. They may tell you that you shouldn't be playing or making so much noise. But remember this: not everyone understands what it is like to be a child who has lost a [relationship]. I am sure that [loved one] would still want you to have fun.

HELP create a child-focused obituary

"The message the child hears is quite clear: Your feelings aren't important; only those of grownups are. Don't bother anyone" (Suzy Yehl Marta).[1]

Obituaries are generally written from an adult perspective to adult readers. Children may have a different perspective in constructing an obituary. Work with the child to create a "child's eye" obituary.

[Name], my [relationship] was born on [date] and died on [date]

1. Favorite sports team
2. Favorite flavor of ice cream
3. Some chores he or she let me do
4. Favorite fun thing to do
5. What I will always remember about [name]
6. What I loved and admired about [name]
7. [Name] had a special nickname
8. One thing [name] always said
9. What did [name's] laugh sound like
10. One thing I will always miss about [name] will be

[Name], an obituary is a small article in the newspaper that tells about the person who has died. It helps a reader understand what was special about the person. Maybe you and I could write an obituary that tells what you think is important about [name].

HONOR the child's anger

"Anger is a common and normal response to grief. It is important to understand that the grieving [child] cannot be forced to accept the loss" (Cheryl Ross Staats, Katherine Pollard, Catherine Brown).[1]

One of the important gifts adults give is to honor the child's anger. Anger may be, initially, the only language in which a child can communicate his or her distress following the loss. The child, depending on the age, may be angry at the deceased in ways that go unnoticed by adults. "He was supposed to take me to the ball game on Saturday" or "Now we can't go to the ball game because we have to go to my grandfather's funeral." The child may be angry at God for taking the loved one (if he or she hears that terminology used). The child may be angry about feeling different from peers in church, school, or the neighborhood. The child may be angry at the loss of predictable routine or security and stability in the home environment.

In some instances, due to violence, the child is angry at a perpetrator of the violence, "That bad man. . . ." especially when the child believes that justice has not been done. "When I get big I am going to get a big gun and kill him!" Anger is often fueled by feelings of powerlessness. Imagine what a child has to process when a parent or sibling is shot by the police. What narratives of the incident is the child hearing? Is the child mimicking the anger of other family members? Imagine what children experience in many of the political hot spots in the world.

Let the child know that you will love him or her despite the expression of anger. I worry more about the child whose anger remains below the surface and erupts in antisocial, aggressive behavior in later years.

Well-meaning individuals may attempt immediately to de-anger the grieving child. "Oh, you shouldn't feel that way!" Do not tell a grieving child how to feel. Do not drag Jesus into the anger management. I suspect Jesus wants to love angry, grieving children through caring adults like you.

It is important for adults to acknowledge and encourage the expression of feelings in appropriate ways. That may be difficult in families that aggressively discourage any expression of anger. Alan Wolfelt suggests that we make an agreement with the angry child: "When I feel like doing this, instead I'll do . . ."

[Name], I know you are angry. If I were you and I had lost [name or relationship], I would be angry too. But even when we are angry, we do not hit or kick or bite. Anytime you are with me, it's OK to express your feelings. [Name], I am always going to love you and care about you.

INCLUDE children in rituals of grieving

"Children who are prepared for the funeral are better able to handle it than those who aren't given prior information. It helps them to feel important and useful at a time when many are feeling overwhelmed" (Norm Wright).[1]

"This helps the child become an identified mourner" (Linda Goldman).[2]

Many parents and grandparents have concluded that children should not attend funeral rituals because it might be too upsetting.

I believe that children are harmed more by being excluded from this important rite of passage. Certainly, it is important to explain to a child before the ritual what will or what *may* happen. For example, some people will be sad, some people will be crying, there will be lots of flowers, and so forth.

At the National Funeral Director's Convention in 2002, author Allison Sims urged the directors to go home and get on their knees in every public space of their facility and imagine what that space would look like and sound like to a grieving child.

Ask the child if he or she wants to attend the ritual. Give him or her some time frame because a child may get restless. Some funeral homes now provide "children's rooms" with videos, books, toys, and art materials.

What many children need is a "ritual buddy" to be a companion during the ritual. Parents may be so overwrought that they overlook the child, particularly if there is a large turnout for the visitation. When John-John became restless during the president's funeral, a sensitive Secret Service Agent took him out and entertained him.

Individuals at visitations often do not know what to say to adults; they are even more nervous in talking to children, especially when there is not a strong existing relationship. Still, make an effort to talk to the child.

Children may need some down time after rituals. A "what did you think?" may be a way to debrief impressions, particularly if it is the child's first funeral or memorial service.

Include the child in planning rituals. In one instance, a child said, "I think we ought to sing Pap-Paw a song." So, during the funeral, the grandchildren came forward, stood by the casket, and confidently sang, "Jesus Loves Me, This I Know" as they had on so many occasions when their grandfather was alive. A child may come up with an idea that unifies the themes of a service.

[Name], I want to tell you how sorry I am that [name] died. [Do not use a cliché or euphemism.] I thought a lot of [name], and I am sure that you will miss him or her a lot. I am glad that so many people have come to say good-bye. And every time I think of you I will pray for you.

JOURNAL your feelings, questions, anxieties

"A journal is not only a record of events that touch and transform us; it is a private space in which we can meet ourselves in relation to others and to God" (Susan Muto).[1]

"Insights that are hazy figures on our horizon sometimes become crystal clear when committed to a journal" (Richard Foster).[2]

Journals offer a sanctuary for ramblings and wonderings. Journals are safe places to rehearse questions. Children sometimes say things or make observations that you think you will always remember, but, in fact, you may forget over time.

By writing down thoughts and impressions a child can acknowledge the impact of the loss. Sometimes a child may offer an insight that ignites a question in your life. Or a child may reboot a question in your heart. Care-ers also need to journal.

Would we know the incident in which Jesus scolded His disciples for turning away children if someone had not observed it, pondered it, told it, and later written it down?

[Name], this is a special book called a journal. It is different from other books because it has no pictures or words in it. But it will after you write in it or paste special pictures in it or draw in it. No one will see this. This is like a special place you can go to be you!

KNOW warning signals

"The path that a child will follow through grief is as unpredictable as children themselves. The best we grownups can do is to be alert to various signs and stages—shock, denial, disbelief, fear, guilt, anxiety, and acceptance—then offer the right words at the right time. Even when children don't show any outward signs of grief, they may still be grieving. Sometimes we need to give permission for grief to be a private and personal matter" (William C. Kroen).[1]

Children, like adults—and perhaps taking signals from adults—learn to camouflage grief so as not to distress others. Spend some moments reviewing this list of warning signals:

1. excessive and prolonged periods of crying
2. frequent and prolonged temper tantrums
3. extreme changes in behavior
4. noticeable changes in school performance and grades
5. withdraw for long periods of time
6. lack of interest in friends and activities they used to enjoy
7. frequent nightmares and sleep disturbances
8. frequent headaches and other physical complaints
9. weight loss or gain
10. apathy, numbness, and a general lack of interest about life
11. prolonged negative thinking about the future, or lack of interest in the future[2]

See Appendix A for another list of red flag behaviors.

Remember language skills are a factor. A child may not be able to tell you about his or her feelings. However, a child knows that saying he has a tummyache may gain immediate attention and may be a bridge into disclosing feelings.

Remember, "Even when children don't show any outward signs of grief, they may still be grieving."[3]

LET this child still be a child

"Children aren't miniature adults. They don't think like adults and don't process information like adults. . . . A child's conscience may be more tender than an adult's conscience. The child doesn't yet have the 'filters' that adults do" (Susan E. Richardson).[1]

Jacqueline Kennedy made a conscious decision for her children not to wear black at their father's funeral. "I want them to look like children," she concluded. Black is not a normal color in a child's wardrobe. Immediately after her husband's death, Martha Custis—later Washington—summoned a dressmaker to make mourning clothes for her and for her children.[2] Let the grieving child wear a favorite item of clothing or one that links him or her to the deceased.

Mrs. Kennedy also took the children's attendance into her decision to ask for a shorter Mass. Even then, John-John was a typical, rambunctious, three-year-old boy. A sensitive Secret Service agent took him out the service and entertained him in the vestibule of the church.

Children grieve intermittently. One minute the child can be somber and the next off playing. That leads some to assume, "He is not grieving." Rather, the child is grieving on his or her own schedule.

Older children worry about being different from their peers. If clothes can make a child feel different, imagine how grief can make them feel odd.

For too many children, the weight of the world seems permanently in their backpack because of a death or a series of deaths or losses. Give the child permission to be a child.

[Name], your responsibility is to be a child. Sometimes, because of what you've been through (or are going through) it can be hard. I admire the way you help your mom (or dad). I think you are a great kid.

LINGER

"Significant adults, persons who relate to children with love and concern, join God in the sacred task of creation . . . Part of our task as persons who nurture children is to be in step with God's timing, a creative pacing divinely led" (Kathyrn N. Chapman).[1]

In the frantic pace of our society, who has "extra" time to be with a child—particularly another individual's child? To really be with a grieving child? Most of our emotional plates are already overflowing. Besides, a grieving child leads some to mumble, "Downer!" A child can sense your impatience to get back to your to-do list.

We bless a child—and ourselves—when we make time to linger with a child.

If Jesus made time in His schedule to be interrupted by children, "to place his hands on them and pray for them" [Matt. 19:13] what further persuasion do you need that God does not consider the emotional needs of children an interruption? Famed children's author Robert Munsch had an extensive correspondence with Gah-Ning, a young reader in Northern Ontario. He surprised her by going to her school to read some of his stories. Afterward, Gah-Ning and her sister, Fone-Ning, told him that they wanted to show him the most important thing in their little town. They showed him their uncle's Chinese restaurant, the toy store, and a large statute of a moose, all of which Munsch initially assumed was "the most important thing in town." Then they walked the author past railroad tracks, through deep snow, and finally stopped in a field. Sticking out of the snow Munsch noticed grave markers. They had brought him to a cemetery. Not just any cemetery, but the cemetery where their grandmother was buried. There Munsch asked, "This wouldn't happen to be the most important thing in town?"

"Absolutely," Gah-Ning replied, followed quickly by her sister's, "No doubt about it."[2]

Munsch only learned what the two young grieving girls considered "the most important thing in town" because he *lingered* long enough for the children to tell him.

[Name], sometimes adults seem to be in a big hurry. But I like just sitting with you. Because if I just sit with you, you may think of some more things you want to tell me about what it is like to be a grieving child. And because something you may teach me will help me help another child.

LOBBY for stability

"Some parents tend to be overly indulgent and forgiving of children because of what the children have been through. This is a mistake" (William C. Kroen).[1]

Children need stability. It has long been considered wise for grievers to not make any major decisions for a year. Unfortunately, in contemporary society, that may be a luxury for the parents of some grieving children. There is a wonderful question that grievers need to ponder before making major decisions, "Is it good for the children?"

I think of a child whose mother died in the World Trade Center. After she divorced she was a single parent of a son for a number of years, and then she married a wonderful man and they had a little girl. During those years, the boy's father made no attempt to contact him or have a relationship. Unfortunately, her new husband had not adopted the boy. Days after the collapse, the biological father appeared to claim the child. Ten days after his mother's death, he was taken away from a secure environment to live with a father he did not know. He lost his mother, his *de facto* stepfather, his half-sister, his home, his school, his church, and his friends. How will that child survive so many losses? What were these people thinking?

As a care-er, you can be a stable factor in a child's life. In fact, in some cases, you may be the only stable influence. Remember this whenever your to-do list suggests that you do not have time for this child. Perhaps tomorrow.

Tomorrow is a long time away for grieving children.

[Name], did your mother ever say, "We will do something tomorrow?" Sometimes, to a great kid like you, tomorrow seems a long time away. Sometimes you will ask, "When is it ever going to be tomorrow?" When we are grieving, we need lots of stability—because that helps us believe in tomorrow. One thing that makes me stable is knowing how much Jesus loves me.

LET a child's curiosity guide the discussion

"One of the things we know through the experiences of many parents and children is that it is better to have all our questions answered, no matter how difficult the answers may be" (Eda LaShan).[1]

How much does a particular child want to know? Some adults have overburdened children with facts and interpretations of facts. Caroline Kennedy wanted to see her father's body. When she was escorted into the East Room of the White House, she was concerned when told that her father was in the casket.

"Daddy's too big for that. How's he lying? Are his knees under his chin?"[2]

Although Caroline wanted to see her father's body, Mrs. Kennedy said no. She did not want Caroline traumatized. But would the child have been traumatized?

[Name], is there anything that you wanted to see or know immediately after the death or during the funeral? Sometimes we adults do not know how to answer your questions, so we just say no or tell you to ask again later. If you think of a question, I will try to answer it or find an answer for it.

MAKE a memory box

"Each one of us has special memories of [the loved one]. You may remember things that I don't remember. I may remember things that you don't remember. That's what's so wonderful about sharing stories, about telling favorite stories" (Bill Dodds).[1]

One important thing you can do for a child is to buy or make a memory box. Better still, create a memory box with the child. Start with a small box like a shoe box or even a plastic container. Ask the child to creatively decorate the outside. Maybe place a photo of the deceased on the outside. Compliment the child on his or her choices. He or she can keep important pictures or memorabilia related to the deceased in the box. You might want to prepare a label on a computer such as "Ryan's Memory Box of His Dad" or "Megan's Precious Memories of Her Sister Karla."

Let the child decide what to place in the box. Take a photo and make a color copy to paste on the outside of the box. The box could contain objects that link the owner to the deceased, or this memory box could be a place to put objects such as drawings or photos or poems or even an obituary.

[Name], I have been thinking that maybe I should contribute something to your memory box for [name]. That way, when you see it, you will remember that other individuals are remembering [name] too. What would you think about that idea?

MAKE lists

"Why lists? Every day of our lives the media bombards us with information through print, TV, CD-ROMS, and the Internet. Lists enable us to make sense of what might otherwise be a mass of data and figures that no one has time to absorb . . . [Lists] help us simplify or organize information in a form that we can easily digest and remember" (Russell Ash).[1]

Lists are tools that help us remember to remember. Many adult grievers have told me that they have to keep a list to keep from forgetting the basics.

Ask the child to create some lists that will jog their memories and stimulate further remembering and reflecting. Here are some samples:

1. Make a list of [name's] favorite foods.
2. Make a list of your favorite memories of [name].
3. Make a list of favorite places you went with [name].
4. Make a list of favorite activities you did with [name].
5. Make a list of states or cities or countries [name] visited.
6. Make a list of individuals [name] admired.[2]
7. Make a list of [name's] favorite books or movies.

Give the child a few moments—or a few hours or days—to work on the list. This assignment may provide an opportunity for conversations with others in order to expand the list. The child may learn some new things about his or her loved one. To enhance the experience, you may want to—if you knew the deceased—make a list and compare it with the child's.

[Name], sometimes I forget things—like I forget to get milk at the store. So I make a list. I was thinking that we could make a list of things to help us remember [name]. What would you think of that idea?

NIP any criticism of the child or the family's grief

"Parents may not have the physical or emotional energy to be of much help to their children . . . Let the children take you by the hand, and learn from them as you seek to help them face their grief" (Andrew Puckett).[1]

In a get-over-it-and-move-on culture, criticism comes in various formats and levels of intensity. In *The Magical Thoughts of Grieving Children*, psychologist James Fogarty describes the common use of magic thought to insulate adults from death and from supporting grieving individuals. Magic thoughts capture the way many American adults want grief to work. Magic thoughts lead to quick-fix admonitions that can sound like criticism to a sensitive child:

"Put it out of your mind!"

"If you let your grief out, your grief will be gone."

"Just believe in God and you will be fine."

"Time heals all wounds."

"Best to get it behind you."[2]

So if an individual, whether adult or a child, is not grieving according to the magical thinking, it is his or her fault because he or she is not trying hard enough to get over the loss. Sadly, some individuals feel free to comment freely on the grief styles of children.

Choose your words carefully. What was never intended as criticism may sound—by the time it gets back to the griever—like criticism. There will be no shortage of opportunities for misunderstanding.

You may remember that Native American wisdom about "walking a mile in my moccasins." William Worden recommends that the child's grieving behaviors be examined in a family context. "The home environment remains the most critical influence on childhood bereavement." If the parent(s) are not adapting well to the loss, the individual or peer support for the child may be severely undercut."[3]

[Name], sometimes, my feelings are hurt by something someone says to me or about me. Some individuals may say some mean words about you or your family's grief. I do not have a right to criticize the way you or your family grieves. If it ever sounds like I am being critical, will you tell me?

NOTICE behavioral changes

"Grief is the emotional and behavior response to loss. It is an emotional reaction that is necessary to maintain quality in both emotional and physical wellbeing. The grieving process involves a total individual experience associated with thoughts, feelings, and behaviors. Grieving related to loss from death is a complex and intense emotional experience" (Judith Allen Shelly and Sharon Fish).[1]

If adults struggle with finding words to describe grief, imagine the pressure on a child to communicate his or her feelings. It should be no surprise that some children regress behavior-wise. Some behaviors signal, "Notice me" or "Pay attention to me." This is not self-centric behavior. How many times do adults say, "I am just not myself." Behavior is a way a child communicates that reality during grief.

Children regress to previous periods of protection and security. They may have a desire to be rocked or nursed or held, they may experience discomfort in being separated from parents; they may resist requests for tasks such as dressing themselves, tying shoes, getting their belongings ready for school. Other children may soil themselves. Some may revert to baby talk or suddenly be afraid of the dark or sleeping alone. Alan Wolfelt is encouraging on this point: "Regressive behaviors in bereaved children are usually temporary. If children are allowed the freedom to return to simpler, safer times, they will usually emerge from their mourning more competent."[2] However, he warns those who do not want to permit children this regression that children may bury the pain within themselves. Then at some future point it will have to be confronted. And what about misbehavior? Wolfelt addresses the issue:

> Unconsciously, grieving children may feel so guilty when someone loved dies that they want to be punished for the death. Acting-out behavior elicits that punishment. The acting-out behavior may even be directed to trying to get the deceased one to come back. They rationalize: "If I'm bad,

Dad will have to come back and make me behave."[3]

The child may be looking for reassurance that you are not going to die and that you are not going to desert him because of misbehavior.

[Name], have you ever heard of a fair-weather friend? That is a friend who likes to be around you when good things are happening but doesn't want to be around you or play with you anymore when things are going badly for you and you're not behaving the way you always did before. That's a fair-weather friend. I know it must be tough on you to lose [name]. But nothing you do can make me love you any less. That doesn't mean I'll just overlook things you do—but I will always love you. No matter what.

OBSERVE special days

"This is the rest of my life, I thought. I knew how much the children would miss Warr. My heart ached for them. I knew about all the birthdays and holidays and graduations when they would see other kids with their fathers. I knew because I'd been there" (Mary Higgins Clark).[1]

In many families, holidays are family time whether it involves a trip, a special holiday meal or treat, or activities like going to the lake or beach as a family. The first holidays without a family member are hard. In the case of the Kennedy children, they immediately faced Thanksgiving and Christmas without the familiar surroundings and support staff of the White House. After a death, some families are reluctant to celebrate holidays. However, Grace Hyslop Christ, a social worker at Columbia University who works with grieving children, believes that observing the holidays and remembering the dead parent or loved one are valuable experiences for children.[2]

Some adults in the family cannot summon sufficient energy to plan and provide a holiday like previous ones; others work feverishly to ignore the loss in order to focus on providing a sensational holiday for the grieving children.

Ask yourself what you can do to help make the spirit of the season or the day intersect with these young grievers. It could be something like making cookies or taking the child to a special Christmas or Fourth of July activity or helping the child buy or wrap some Christmas presents or pick out a Valentine. Baby-sitting might be a welcomed practical gift. Or maybe there is some musical program at your church that the child would enjoy.

[Name], I have been wondering if you have some ideas on how you would like to celebrate the upcoming holiday. Is there something I could do to help you?

PLAY with the child

"Kids use play to understand their worries, fears, and concerns" (Joan Schweizer Hoff and Amy Lindholm).[1]

"Children who do not openly display their sadness or sense of loss often will reveal it through play. Themes of family loss and death may surface as they play with dolls or action figures, or as they act out home or school roles with friends; for example they might 'lose' a parent figure doll" (William C. Kroen).[2]

Phillips Brooks, once pastor of the historic Trinity Church in Boston, had a reputation as one of the greatest American preachers. He loved children and composed the lyrics for the Christmas classic "O Little Town of Bethlehem." A great believer in pastoral calling, one afternoon he knocked on a door and a child answered. The child explained that his parents were not home but were expected soon, so Pastor Brooks decided to wait for them. In the meantime, when the child invited him to play, the 350-pound pastor got down on the living room floor and played with the child. Imagine the parents' surprise when they came home and found the senior minister of their church on the floor engaged joyously in a children's game.

Games are important because they build relationships. Games ignite conversations. A child may not come out and say, "I want to talk about . . ." but, at play, the question might come up or the observation might be offered. Sometimes it is not the initial statement that is significant but what the child says after you ask, "What makes you say [or think] that?"

Playgrounds are great places for grieving children—especially when the grieving parent cannot take them as often as the children want. I love words offered by the late Mr. Rogers: "When we treat children's play as seriously as it deserves, we are helping them feel the joy that's to be found in the creative spirit. We're helping ourselves stay in touch with that spirit too." He nudged adults, "It's the things we play with and the people who help us play that make a great difference in our lives."[3]

[Name], I would like to play a game with you. What game would you like to play?

PRAY for and with the child

"More things are wrought through prayer than this world imagines" (Alfred Lord Tennyson).[1]

Children have no problem putting into practice the words of Joseph Scovern, in the hymn "Sweet Hour of Prayer," "Take it to the Lord in prayer." I recently spent time in the prayer chapel of Christ United Methodist Church in Memphis. As I flipped through the pages of prayer requests, one entry in a child's handwriting caught my attention: "[Pray] for Grandmother to have a long-lived life and to keep my dead grandfather with her in her heart!" signed "Tray." I wish I could have talked with Tray to discover what was behind his prayer request. In a "get over it" culture, was he afraid that his grandmother would forget his grandfather? Had he overheard someone say that?

Elizabeth Reed reminds us that "children have warm hearts; it is natural for them to pray for those whom they love. And it will help them to continue to remember in their prayers the person they loved who has died."[2] This may be particularly true with many Hispanic children around the time of the celebration of Day of the Dead in early November.

Children have a spectrum of attitudes about prayers that "did not work." One morning, a seven-year-old boy fervently prayed, "Jesus, do not let anything happen to my mother." (His mother was in a hospital, but the child did not know she was in a psychiatric unit.) That afternoon when the boy came home from school his father informed him that his mother had suffered a heart attack and died. In fact, she had committed suicide, although it would be years before the boy learned that detail. That boy, as an adult, recalled the day: "It was Friday, April 14. Jesus had failed me. Jesus had let me down. Jesus forgot my prayer about Mother. I was too young to know that little in life was fair . . . I never asked Jesus for anything again." The young boy was actor Peter Fonda.[3]

Some children will listen closely to what is said about

prayer, particularly if they expected the individual to get better or well.

It's easy for some people to ask a child, "Did you say your prayers?" Rather than asking children if they prayed, remind them that they can pray anytime, anyplace.

1. Pray *with* the child. Listening to a child's prayers—particularly at bedtime or mealtime—may provide an opportunity for discussion.

2. Pray *for* the child. Every time that child comes to mind, breathe a prayer for him or her. One of the gifts you can give a grieving child is to pray for that child by name and to tell him or her that you are praying specifically for him or her as well as for the family.

Then ask the Lord to bring that child to mind. You might create a song, making up the melody:

> *I'll be praying for you,*
> *I'll be praying for you.*
> *Every time you come to mind,*
> *I will mention you to God.*

[Name], all this must be hard for you to understand. I want you to know that every time you come to mind—which will be quite often—I will pray for you. I will mention your name to Jesus. And He will help you.

PLANT something

"The tree represents a new life and a living tribute to the deceased. Whenever your children see 'Daddy's tree,' it will bring back fond memories of the times they spent with him. As your children grow and become strong, so will the tree. Let them know the reason for planting the tree, and point out how you feel when you look at it" (William C. Kroen).[1]

Ask the child to help you choose something to plant in memory of his or her loved one. Ask the child—with the permission of the parent(s)—for ideas about where to plant a bush, a plant, even a tree. When you do the planting, have the child write a message or a poem or draw a picture and bury that in the soil with the tree. Or ask the child to write his or her name on a small rock to bury in the soil or place around the tree or plant.

If the child lives in a home that may not be permanent, you may want to think about doing the planting at school or at church or in a special place that has meaning to the child.

As an alternative, Wolfelt suggests that you buy a houseplant for the child to keep in his or her room. Get one that will need little upkeep—cactuses and succulents survive on little water.[2]

[Name], do you know who planted the first tree? God did. I think God likes plants and trees and shrubs and bushes because He made so many of them. Someday, you can come back here and be amazed at how tall and big this tree or plant has grown or how beautiful it is, and you will remember the day we planted it.

PRESERVE the past

"There was sort of the removal of everything 'her' from the house in some kind of tragically wrong 1970s version of grieving that my father partook in. There was nothing left. I only have two pictures of her and none of her things. No jewelry, nothing" (James Robert Parish).[1]

Some individuals hurry to dispose of the personal belongings of the deceased. For a child, that "cleansing" (or just losing the object temporarily) and the loss of familiar objects linked to the deceased can be distressing. A few days after her mother's death, one daughter came home from school and found that the house had been stripped of everything that had been her mother's. She remembered that it was like losing her mother all over again.

It may be necessary to do some initial disposing of personal effects. But the question should be pondered: How will this affect this child? One individual took the child for a visit to the park while some things were disposed of. However, because they came home early, they found piles of black trash bags full of his father's belongings at the curb. That experience was significantly distressing.

Suggest that a parent store some items in case the child wants the items later. If there is a yard sale, you might purchase an item to link you to the child and the deceased.

Michael Mayne was three years old when his father, a minister, committed suicide by jumping from the church belfry. In those days of harsh reaction to suicide, Mayne's mother was "left homeless and virtually penniless." A person who committed suicide was allowed no marked grave or memorial. His father's ashes were "scattered to the four winds, and nobody spoke of him again." Imagine the shock on the boy.

Sixty years later, after Michael had become the dean of St. Paul's Cathedral in London, someone in his father's church decided there should be some effort at reconciliation. So, on Mrs. Mayne's 94th birthday, with her children, grandchildren, and great-grandchildren, the family made a pilgrimage back for a service of remembrance. Michael Mayne, who does not remember his father, was touched that some individuals in the congregation brought photocopied newspaper stories for the family—many containing details Mayne had never known.

That preservation of the past gave Mayne a chance to revisit the loss and to conclude, "I believe that when he fell to his death he was at the deepest sense caught and held in the everlasting arms of the one who is the merciful and loving Father of us all."[2]

Make no mistake, there may be some distant day when this child will be more able to treasure some document, some relic, some trinket from the past.

[Name], do you have anything that belonged to [name]? If you could have anything that belonged to [name], what would it be? What would you do with it?

PROCESS media coverage

"11 kids die needlessly" "Community mourns 10-year-old drive-by victim" (headlines in the *Kansas City Star*).

Children could once be shielded from the news. Today's reality is ongoing, unsupervised media exposure to "breaking" news stories and the media fascination with disasters and tragedies through ongoing coverage. Countless children watched the coverage of the Oklahoma City bombing and the collapse of the World Trade Center towers. In fact, the major media stopped rerunning the footage of the planes crashing into the towers because children were believing that more buildings were being attacked and collapsing.

As I write this I am looking at a front page of the *Kansas City Star*, and what I am about to say applies to any major metropolitan newspaper or *USA Today*. Newspapers often use what I call "sob" pictures—pictures that catch the eye placed above the fold line to be visible where newspapers are sold—of the tragic and the heartbreaking. Today, under the caption "A final goodbye," is a full-color picture of a child being held up to close the casket lid of his murdered brother. (The child's mother and her boyfriend have been charged with child abuse.) How many adults turned away from the picture or quickly moved on to page 2 or to the sports section? Yet, children notice pictures not just in newsstands but on coffee tables and sofas or kitchen tables, in libraries, in the trash.

It is not so much the information that confuses the child but how the information is interpreted or misinterpreted—particularly if accompanied by adult silence. In one study of Boston children, following the September 11 terrorism, many school administrators were ill prepared to make decisions on initial coverage. In some schools, the information was broadcast over the loudspeaker; some children watched on classroom televisions. In other schools, the news was initially kept from the children. Either way, 88.2 percent of older school-age children knew something about the devastation by the time they reached home that afternoon. Children who did not hear about it in the classroom learned on the school bus or on the way home. Some parents who went to pick up their children at school discovered their children already had an awareness of the tragedy.[1]

[Name], sometimes adults say things without thinking about how a kid will hear those words. You may hear lots of things that frighten you. Whenever radio or television news frightens you, you can ask God to help you not be so frightened. Or you can ask an adult, like your parent(s) or me what is going on. You know, sometimes things happen that frighten me and I just say a bunch of words. Later, I wonder, now why did I say that? It may have been because I did not want to admit that I was frightened.

QUESTION the child gently

"Curiosity killed the cat" (American proverb).

"Inquiring minds want to know . . ." captures the American fascination with curiosity, which some have developed into an art form. Yes, adults want to know "and how are the children doing?" following loss. However, many stop asking and begin complimenting. Rather than asking the child or the parent, "How are you doing?" they say, "You are doing so well."

The danger is coming at children with the questioning skills of lawyer Johnny Cochran. Rather, wise questions may be more like breadcrumbs.

William Worden believes that if a loved one has died as a result of suicide, caring adults need to be direct with the child: "Have you thought about harming yourself?"[1]

Before you unleash questions, build trust with this child.

[Name], sometimes I ask questions because I am curious. But sometimes I may ask questions so you can help me better understand what it is like to be you. You may want to think about the answer for a while.

READ to or with the child

"What is the use of a book, thought Alice, without pictures or conversations?" (Alice).[1]

Children's books can be a valued resource in building bridges into the grief of a child. C. S. Lewis, no stranger to grief, having lost his mother at age eight, in the movie *Shadowlands* asked a student to respond to the statement, "We read to know we are not alone." Would Lewis have become a great writer had he not sought refuge *within* his grief—not *from* his grief—in reading?

1. Read *to* a child. Some resources are best read to a child, depending on reading level and comprehension. My favorite grief-themed children's book is *Nadia the Willful*. Nadia, maybe age seven, refuses to go along with her father's order to the tribe never to again speak about her brother, Hamed, lost in a desert sandstorm. Although Tarik threatens to banish anyone who even says Hamed's name, Nadia "the willful" becomes the one who remembers. Finally, in an angry confrontation with her father she yells, "You will not rob me of my brother Hamed! I will not let you!" Eventually, after Tarik calms, she began to speak of Hamed. She told of walks she and Hamed had taken and of talks they had. She told how he had taught her games, told her tales, and calmed her when she was angry. She told him many things that she remembered, some happy and some sad."[2]

Based on his daughter's persistence and example, Tarik learns ways to remember his son, and he changes his daughter's name to "Nadia the Willful."

In many families the demand to not remember or not talk openly about the deceased loved one is more subtly communicated. Either way, the child is twice robbed: once by the death and then robbed of an environment to remember the deceased.

Reading to a child leads to the question, "What do you think?" which can jump-start insightful conversations.

2. Read *with* a child. In some cases, you might want to "plant" a book with an idea and let the child read to you. When

you read aloud, other children in the room—seemingly doing their own thing—nevertheless hear and store away some of the reading.

3. Read *for* a child. Spend some time in a bookstore or the children's section of a library looking for books to share with a child.

4. Consider writing a book about the loss with a child. Ask the child to write a story about a child who has experienced a significant loss. With computer graphics, you might find a resource that would help the child and other children. For example, readers have *The Living Bible* (Tyndale) today because Ken Taylor translated Scripture into words his children could understand.

Books can be gifts of healing for children and for adults. Make sure your local public library, elementary school libraries, and church libraries have copies of resources listed in Appendix C and Appendix D. In fact, you could donate copies of these wonderful resources as a memorial gift that would have long-term blessing for future grieving children.

[Name], when I listened to you read—and you read very well —I was thinking that I miss your [mom/sister/grandmother]. I bet she was proud of how well you read. Sometimes when I am sad I look for just the right book. Books can be like special friends for grieving children that help you understand that other children have grieved.

RESPOND to the child's fears or anxieties

"If you're not safe in church, where are you safe? If you can't go to church and not worry about getting killed, where can you go?" (Bernice King after witnessing her grandmother's death; Dexter King).[1]

For months after Mrs. King's death—and for the five years after the death of her father and her uncle—the youngest King child flipped through the family photo albums, asking, "I wonder who's next?" That's significant anxiety for a child to bear. Unfortunately, some children are not immune to a string of losses that leads them to wonder: "Who's next?"

I heard about a child who once told his Sunday School teacher, "I used to be afraid of mice. But Jesus gave me a non-afraid feeling." One important goal is to give children permission to pray their grief and fears, some of which they may be unable to verbalize.

It is too tempting to disenfranchise the child's fear by insisting that he or she "act big" or by belittling the fear, "Why, there's nothing to fear." If you acknowledge the child's fear, you may be more likely to get at what is motivating the fear. Fears resemble icebergs. There is the fear of sleeping alone, but below the emotional surface of the child are equally menacing fears. Listening to the child's statement of fear is building a bridge into the other under-the-radar fears that may be operating or about to kick into gear.

Grief can raise lots of fears in some children, particularly if a loved one died as an act of violence or homicide. There may be legal issues if both parents die—particularly without a will. Imagine what the Simpson children feared following the death of their mother, Nicole Simpson, and the murder trial of their father, O. J. Simpson. These children may have an enhanced fear that the "surviving" parent will also die.

Some children may acknowledge fears or anxieties to you before they will disclose them to a parent or grandparent. Every child has things that go bump in the night.

Sensitive, caring care-ers may respond by sharing an experience from their own memories of childhood anxieties. You may want to read Robert Munsch's classic book *Love You Forever*. Or ask the child to sing the words from the carol "Away in the Manger":

> *Be near me Lord Jesus, I ask Thee to stay*
> *Close by me forever and love me I pray.*
> *Bless all the dear children in Thy tender care*
> *And fit us for heaven, to live with Thee there.*
>   —John Thomas McFarland

Although categorized as a "Christmas hymn," these words may have particular meaning for a grieving child.

[Name], when I was about your age, I used to worry about [or be afraid of] . . . One thing that helps me today when I am afraid—and adults still get afraid—is to tell God about it. You can tell God anything.

RESIST the temptation to try to "make it all better"

"The ordinary response for many to such atrocities is to banish the terror from existence. However, avoiding the topic doesn't make it go away, as we have learned from other more familiar traumas such as child abuse and domestic violence" (Michelle A. Beauchesne).[1]

"I remember more than anything the coffins. The small coffins. And the sense that Birmingham wasn't a very safe place" (Condoleeza Rice).[2]

Birmingham was rocked by the bomb blast that shattered the Sixteenth Avenue Baptist Church and sent chunks of concrete the size of footballs hurtling through the air. Four children died that September Sunday morning in 1963 as Sunday School began. Angelina and John had insulated their daughter from many of the injustices of segregation. The bombing, however, was a challenge they could not fix. Denise McNair, their daughter's friend, had died. Their daughter would never forget walking into the joint funerals, tightly clinging to her parents' hands. Nor would she forget the stirring words of Martin Luther King Jr. in the funeral sermon, "[The children] didn't live long lives, but they lived meaningful lives. Their lives were distressingly small in quantity, but glowingly large in quality."[3]

The little girl was Condoleeza Rice. By not trying to fix the loss, the Rices gave their daughter a gift: permission to wrestle with the injustices of life and with her grief for a friend. As a result, a leader developed who would provide decisive leadership. Her calm coolness after September 11 was a testimony of her parents' unwillingness to "fix" her grief. She told the graduating class at Stanford University in 2002, "Though I didn't see [the bombing], I heard it a few blocks away. And it is a sound that I can still hear today. Those memories of Birmingham bombings have flooded back to me since September 11. And, as I watched the conviction of the last conspirator in the church bombing last month, I realized now that it is an experience that I have overcome but will never forget."[4]

It is tempting to want to take actions to "make it all better" for the child or to "fix" the child's grief or to urge the child to forget. Wise parents helped Condoleeza learn from the traumatic loss. The wisdom of a TV commercial challenges such well-meaning desires. The Fram Auto Filter commercial reminds viewers: "You can pay me now, or you can pay me later." A grief delayed is a grief compounded.

There are three questions a compassionate companion should ponder:

1. What can I do?
2. What can I *not* do?
3. What can I do *now*?

[Name], there are some things I can fix and some things I cannot fix. I wish I had a magic wand and could take away all the pain you have experienced. But I cannot. What I know is that sometimes bad things happen to neat kids, but God finds ways to comfort us and to make us stronger because of it.

REMEMBER together

"I expect sometimes that helping our children through sorrow is as much for our good as it is for theirs" (Maureen Rank).[1]

Psychologists are clear that we do not have to "forget" those we have loved. Grief specialist Alan Wolfelt has long insisted that an active memory enhances healing. One way to keep up a child's memory skills is to remember together. That may be done on walks or while playing or at the cemetery or at bedtime.

It could almost become a version of the game "I Spy." "I remember something that you do not remember and one hint is . . . " This is an important activity because it helps jog the memory, it demonstrates that family members remember individuals and incidents differently, and it refreshes details of a memory.

Here are some ideas you might try:

Try to remember how [name] laughed.

Try to remember how [name] hugged.

Try to remember how [name] scolded or teased.

Try to remember what [name] said after a good meal.

Try to remember [name's] favorite food or dessert.

Try to remember the best present [name] ever gave you.

Try to remember the best present you ever gave [name].

Admittedly, this can become a troublesome issue if a surviving parent remarries and if the new spouse intends to be the mother or father replacement. Some children have stealth memories that need an outsider to hear, share, and appreciate. It can be troublesome if a new spouse or partner (remember several million children live in coupled nonmarital relationships) begins removing memory links such as pictures or particular pieces of furniture that belonged to the deceased or takes down or puts away pictures of the deceased.

[Name], some people think that remembering makes us sad. I don't. I think remembering help us. What do you think?

SEND cards

"When you send a card out at an unexpected time, it stands out. It creates a bigger memory" (Suzanne C. Ryan).[1]

"Keep in mind the recipient's values, religious beliefs and maturity when sending a greeting" (Shanna Bartlett Groves).[2]

Many adults send family sympathy cards, "To the family of Jim Adams." One gift to a grieving child is to send a card specifically for him or her. Admittedly, you may have to spend time looking for a card that the child can understand. You may choose a card with white space inside and create a message for this child. Ask yourself: What could I say that would encourage this child through this difficult time?

A high percentage of sympathy cards are sent during the initial bereavement, perhaps 30 days, when friends are uncomfortable knowing what to say. The child may especially value cards that come at various times or the "just thinking of you today cards."

You also might want to note on your calendar special days such as the child's birthday, the anniversary of the death, Christmas, or Easter. Ann Landers once counseled her readers that some who are grieving need "someone to visit with, so instead of mailing a condolence card, take it to them."[3] The card may jump-start a conversation.

Shanna Bartlett Groves suggests, "Treat each greeting card like you would a personal gift. Let it be a meaningful expression of your feelings" for the grieving child. Through this card communicate why this child is special to you.[4]

[Name], a card is a way of saying, I may not know what to say, but I am thinking of you.

SHOW UP for special and routine events in the child's life

"I went out to watch Andrew play baseball. He played a particularly good game that day. Afterward I said, 'Oh, I wish Buppy could have seen you play today.' He looked me in the eye and said matter-of-factly, 'Oh, he did. He and Gramma Hazel (Harold's mother) always watch me play. They even help me catch the ball.' His certainty about spiritual things helped my faith. I held on to Harold's and Andrew's trust in God" (Ethel Young).[1]

I learned a significant lesson from my friend, Fred Sykes, who has a long experience in ministry with children. He told me that he could not do something because he had to go to a soccer game.

"Is it a championship game or something?" I asked.

"No, just a regular game, but I want the child to know I am as interested in him on a Tuesday afternoon as I am on Sunday morning. And it gives me a little time to focus one-on-one attention where on Sunday mornings I have to think of all the children in my ministry."

You may not be able to stay for the whole game, recital, or play. But make sure the child knows that you were there.

If you cannot attend, call afterward and find out about the event.

Follow up with a phone call or note or e-mail, "I sure was proud of you last week." In the church world, individuals can conveniently demonstrate an interest in the child on Sunday morning in the context of Sunday School or children's church. But the child knows and appreciates when you go out of your way to interact with him or her.

[Name], how do you feel when you see the parents of other kids at [name an event]? Does it make you feel sad or mad or bad?

TALK about all kinds of things

"Let children talk about the disaster and ask questions as much as they want. Encourage children to describe what they are feeling. Children's fears may also stem from their imaginations, and these feelings need to be taken seriously. Children need help sorting out fact from fiction to perceive a realistic picture of what has occurred" (Tenner Goodwin Veenema).[1]

Conversations with children sometimes resemble a breadcrumb trail: You never know where the conversation will lead. Talking about something that seemingly has nothing to do with the loss the child has experienced may, circuitously, lead to the loss. Give the conversation time to meander.

You help a child when you talk about all kinds of things and not just about issues related to the child's loss and grief. You might ask, "OK, what do you want to talk about today?" If the child is hesitant, say, "What about rhinos?" If the child objects, then say, "All right, you pick a topic." Or you can alternate picking topics for conversation.

Or you might write potential topics on index cards in large letters. Then let the child pick a card and a topic. One topic might be dogs or school or ice cream or the loved one's death. Start out with 10 cards. You do not have to cover all of them in one setting. Or the child could pick a card and then you would have to begin the conversation on that topic. Suppose he draws "Dogs." You might begin, "You know, in some places in Ireland, when someone dies, a child is chosen to tell the dogs about the death."

By talking about a variety of topics, you may get some hints how the child is integrating the loss. And as conversations do, one thing may lead to another and you may find the child opening up. Otherwise, the sensitive child may conclude, "The only thing he wants to talk about is death or grief!"

Remember this is a grieving child who has lots of other things going on in his or her life.

Sometimes a child may not want to talk at all. Sometimes it is just good to hang out with a child.

[Name], I enjoy talking to you. You teach me things from a child's point of view. I like to talk to you, and I hope you like to talk to me. I hope you will feel free to talk to me anytime about anything.

TELL the truth

"When speaking about death and grieving to your children, truth and honesty are always the best approaches. Being truthful and honest is not the same as being blunt and insensitive. You can talk about death and grieving in a warm, caring, sensitive way" (William C. Kroen).[1]

"A part of honesty means using the real words. Say *died* and *dead.* Saying *passed away* or *passed on* or just plain *gone* could be confusing to children. The more you use *dead* and *died,* the more understandable it becomes and is easier for them to accept reality" (Joy Johnson and Earl Grollman).[2]

Truth-telling does not take place all at once. William Kroen explains, "It will probably take many quiet, serious, compassionate conversations with your children to help them understand death."[3]

This is especially true when the death has a stigma. You may know, believe, suspect that the deceased died from suicide. What do you tell the child? One eight-year-old instructed a center counselor not to tell his mother the truth about his father's suicide, because "she thinks he died in an accident."[4] Joan Schweizer Hoff and Amy Lindholm, staff members of the Dougy Center in Portland, Oregon—an exemplary center for grieving children—discount the wish of parents to protect a child from the truth. Rather, they argue, children deserve to know the truth "and, on some level, do know."

Prayerfully ponder what you should say to a grieving child. Talk to the parent(s) or grandparent(s).

[Name], telling the truth is always important. Some adults will think that because you are a child you should not be told everything. I promise you that I will never lie or mislead you. I will always do my best to be honest with you.

UTILIZE resources specifically designed for children

"By exploring the feelings we may have regarding the death of a loved one and the ways to remember someone after he or she has died, [books] can serve as a comfort to children and families at a difficult time in their lives" (Introduction to *When Dinosaurs Die*).[1]

One of the best resources for discussing death with children is *When Dinosaurs Die: A Guide to Understanding Death*, written by Laurie Krasny Brown and Marc Brown. The text of the book, supported by creative art, provides answers to some of the most commonly asked questions children ponder:

- What does "alive" mean?
- What does "dead" mean?
- What comes after death?

Two features in the book are particularly helpful: "Ways to remember someone" and the glossary of terms. Purchase a copy to give to this child and make sure that copies of this book are in your church library and in your school library. Admittedly, some evangelical Christians may raise eyebrows at the section, "What comes after death?" because it presents a variety of ideas held in today's pluralistic society. However, rather than discard the resource, it becomes a way to discuss what other families and religions believe. If a child's classmate or family member dies, she might belong to another world religion or to a family that has no belief in afterlife.

Before you give any resource, read through it or ask for the recommendation (or qualifiers) from a children's minister, librarian, elementary school teacher, or a therapist who works with children.

The Centering Corporation, founded in 1977 by Joy and Marvin Johnson, has developed more than 150 resources for grieving children. They also carry a wide line of other grief resources, some in Spanish. Centering Corporation has also developed a special "healing hearts pillow" designed to bring comfort and healing to a child.

The Center Corporation
402-553-1200
Centeringcorp@aol.com or www.centering.org
Compassion Books
www.compasionbooks.com
1-800-970-4229

One particularly helpful resource developed by Alan Wolfelt for Compassion Books is "My Grief Rights," a poster and wallet cards for kids. These products help grieving kids understand their feelings and empower them to mourn in healthy ways.

Dr. Alan Wolfelt
Center for Grief and Loss Recovery
www.centerforloss.com
Companion Press
970-226-6050

If there are insufficient resource books—or only one copy—available at your school or public library, you might want to make a donation to buy additional copies in honor of the deceased.

[Name], I found some wonderful books written for children who are grieving. Something in a book might be helpful to you. Would you like to read one with me?

VISIT the child

"For I was in [grief] and you came to visit me" (Matt. 25:36).

"I closed the door, switched off the light, and flopped down across my bed. I remember crying quietly for a few minutes lying there in the darkness thinking about Dad, wishing he hadn't died, wondering what his death would mean to our life together as a family. Then suddenly there was a quiet tapping on the door. One of my mother's sisters entered the bedroom and sat down beside me. She didn't say anything. She just sat beside me with her hand resting on my shoulder. I wondered if my mother had sent her. I think I'll always remember how much my aunt's silent, loving presence meant in that time of grief" (Jerry Falwell).[1]

Jesus' words in Matthew might be paraphrased, "For I was grieving and you visited me." The child can be blessed by you visiting him or her. The child generally will feel more comfortable with you on his or her own turf. Immediately following the death, the child may want to show you pictures of the deceased or flowers that have been sent or cards received. These can be conversation jump-starters.

For another child, a neutral site like McDonald's could make conversation more relaxed.

The visit does not have to be long to be effective.

Because housekeeping may be one of the things that goes by the wayside as a family grieves, call ahead to arrange a time to visit. You may need to remind a grieving parent who you are and your intent in visiting the child.

[Name], I wanted to drop by and see you. I find myself thinking about you often and praying that God will help you. Grief is a big, big job. I know the death of [name] must be very hard for you.

VISIT the cemetery or scattering area

"Plan the trip to the gravesite in advance. The length of time you stay can be short; 10 minutes may be enough. You or [the] child can take flowers and place them on the grave. Flowers gathered from your yard or from a nearby field are always nice. Graves are also good places to leave notes . . . perhaps dealing with some unfinished business you or your child may have with the deceased" (Helen Fitzgerald).[1]

Unfortunately, cemeteries are a low priority for many individuals. Thus, a child's first encounter with a cemetery may be the burial of a loved one. This is part of our society's denial of death.

Some children may take their clues from family members who dislike visiting the cemetery. They may remember experiences in which the parent(s) broke down and cried—so the child may be trying to avoid that happening. With you, the experience could be totally different. Helen Fitzgerald counsels:

I believe you should give your child the opportunity to return to the gravesite at least once after the burial, just to see if it is helpful. Does your child find it comforting to be near the loved one? Or does it mean nothing?[2]

Since a child cannot drive and a parent may not want to visit when the child does, you can offer a gift to the child by volunteering to drive him or her or go along to visit the cemetery.

As a child I visited my cousins who lived across the street from the cemetery. On more than one occasion we stopped playing to observe Clarence Gilbaugh, the town's funeral director, leading a funeral procession toward a grave. The experience was natural to my cousins—so it became natural to me.

Some children will want to go to the cemetery, even on special days. This is a great opportunity to ask a child to do a drawing or make a card to take to the grave. Sometimes standing or sitting on a grave for a few moments can give a chance to swap some memories or talk.

Sometimes cemeteries have rules about leaving objects or memory gifts on graves. I have taken an idea from my friend Nancy Keller: use glitter. Dust the grave with glitter every time you go. Throw the glitter high into the air over the grave. On a sunny day, it is a wonderful visual experience. When Nancy's mother died, vials of glitter were passed out at the cemetery. We were asked to come forward and toss a handful over Dorothy Culver's casket. The children—and many of the adults—loved it.

Another way of introducing children to cemeteries is to visit the graves of presidents or local heroes and historical personalities.

In the cemetery where the child's loved one is buried, there may be some famous or colorful individuals buried. Ask at the cemetery office. You may be surprised by stories waiting to be told.

[Name], some children do not like to go to a cemetery because they are afraid they will become sadder. But sometimes in a cemetery we can say things we cannot say elsewhere. I do not think they can hear us up in heaven, but God can always hear us—and that is what is important. Also, sometimes memories come to our minds in a cemetery that will make us feel sad and good at the same time.

VALUE the child's faith wonderings

"How old is Dad?" he [my son] asked me one night. "He doesn't have an age now." "Why?" "Because when you die, sweetie, you don't have any more birthdays." "No birthdays? No birthday parties in heaven?" He frowned (Ana Veciana-Suarez).[1]

Death is difficult for adults to accept; its finality is more absolute than anything we know. Imagine then what it must be like for children, little ones who have yet to distinguish between fantasy and fact, between a talking Scooby-Doo and the neighbor's Great Dane. "During the first years of his life, Nicholas's [age three. when his father died] little brain worked hard to make sense of conversations he overheard and events he observed, and I swear that when we spoke, I could see his mental gears moving, pulling, struggling to grasp these complex concepts."[2]

Robert Benson was baby-sitting a young boy who asked, "Do you know what happens to us when we die?" Robert noted that the child "had that look that told me he knew the answer and that if I would resist the urge to pull some grown-up theological reasoning on him he would let me in on his secret." Robert patiently waited "for both the answer and for him to finish the cookie."

"Well," the boy said, "God breaks them up into little pieces and takes the best parts of us and makes other people out of them." This was a new theory to Robert.

"How do you know?" Robert asked offhandedly.

"God told me one night when I was asleep."[3]

Children's wonderings about faith and death can resemble an iceberg: about 10 percent is above the water line and about 90 percent is below. By honoring the 10 percent the child expresses, you may receive an invitation from the child to explore some of the more troubling questions, anxieties, or wonderings.

The important gift is for children to have permission to voice their wonderings and their conclusions in a safe, caring environment. You can work to create a safe environment by taking a child to a playground or on a walk and by intentionally listening to whatever a child wants to tell you.

Some adults, unfortunately, pounce on the theological absurdity in Benson's experience. After that correction, the child would probably never share with that adult—or perhaps any adult—again.

[Name], I learn a lot from talking to you. I think it is OK to wonder about God. Sometimes I say, "God, why did You let this happen?" I thought that when [name] died. God knows how sad we are when we have lost someone we love.

WRITE a poem or story or bumper sticker together

"Each time a child describes an experience he or she or someone else has had, he or she constructs part of the past, adding to the sense of who he or she is and conveying that sense to others . . . The stories we tell, whether they are about real or imagined events, convey our experiences, our ideas, a dimension of who we are" (Susan Engel).[1]

"Storytelling is as ancient as human civilization" (Donna O'Tolle).[2]

Grieving children have been telling and listening to stories as long as humankind has existed. Many children find writing a story or a poem a creative way to rehearse their grief. Clearly, many poems cherished by adult grievers have vocabulary or imagery too complex for children. So you might want to say to a child, "Let's write a poem about your loved one or about your experience of grief." Offer the child a first line to jump-start the poem:

"Grief came knocking at my door one day . . ."

"I keep hoping that one of these days . . ."

"Someday I won't feel so sad because . . ."

Ask the child to repeat the line several times before beginning to write. Join in the creativity of making a poem with a child. The creative process may lead to more conversation.

As an alternative approach, Alan Wolfelt suggests that the child write the deceased's name vertically on a sheet of paper. Ask the child to begin each line of the poem with a word with the corresponding letter.[3]

This needs to be the child's creative effort. Your task is to be the scribe listening to or writing down what the child is saying or thinking (rather than editing or coercing the child's words).

Ask the child to create a story. Norm Wright offers this as a way to jump-start a story-creating experience. Tell the child you are going to share a story with him or her. And have the child help create the story. Begin with this story fragment:

"There is a little girl whose best friend knocks on the door. 'Can you come over to my house and play?'"

"No," the little girl answers. "I have to go to a memorial service because _____ died." Who died? How do you think this little girl feels about not being able to play with her friend? What does her friend say to her?

Or to address fears or anxieties the child-griever has, you could begin the story: "There was a child, whose _____ had died. One day, sitting in the swing in the park, he said to himself, 'Oh, I am so afraid.'" Ask the child: "What do you think this little boy was afraid of?" Norm adds follow-up questions:

What does being afraid do to us?

Why are children afraid?

What can we do about this fear?[4]

An older child might create a bumper sticker. Fold a sheet of copy paper in half and ask the child what would sound good enough to put on the bumper of the family car.

William Worden reminds us to be cautious of privacy issues and to obtain the permission of the child "if the material is to be shared with others."[5]

[Name], I like the way you use words. Sometimes, it is hard for me to find just the right words. So this is like practicing the words. Anytime you want to share a poem or a story with me, I would be honored to read it.

WRITE a letter to the child

"Dear Daddy, We are all going to miss you. Daddy, I love you very much. Caroline Kennedy (Letter placed in John Kennedy's casket).[1]

In the first grade, I cried every day on the school bus. (If you had had my first grade teacher you would have cried too!) The other kids laughed at me. Then I got a letter (my first) from my Sunday School teacher, Alberta Jones: "Dear Harold, I hear you are having a hard time going to school. You know, I think Jesus really wants you to be a big boy and like school." I stopped crying. I began to like school—even with my teacher. I have never forgotten that letter.

In these days of instant communication, phone or e-mail, we overlook the lasting importance of a letter that can be read and reread and treasured.

Take some time to craft a letter to a child. You might open a letter with one of the following statements:

[Name], I have been praying for you (or thinking about you). It must be hard to be a kid and lose [name or relationship].

[Name], you are helping me understand what it is like to be a grieving child.

[Name], I think children like you are a lot braver than many adults realize. Since [name or relationship] died it's been hard on you, but you have been so good (or you have continued to do well in school or you have taken on more responsibilities).

YOU can make a difference in this child's life

"Like Peter Pan, there are untold numbers of adults in the world who, in some important way, have never grown up. They never had a chance to resolve the grief, the sadness, the sense of terrible loss they suffered as children when someone very important to them was taken from them by death. They have remained in this time warp, not because their loved ones died, but because the adults around them, perhaps consumed by their own grief, failed to see how shattered they were or how much they needed to express their grief" (Helen Fitzgerald).[1]

Most readers have loved—at some point in their lives—James Barrie's *Peter Pan*. Had Scottish-born Barrie had a normal childhood, there might never have been a Peter Pan. Barrie, born the 9th of 10 children, early in life heard stories of pirates from his mother, who read selections from Robert Lewis Stevenson to her children at night. Mrs. Barrie, devoutly religious, wanted David, her "favorite" child, age 14, to become a minister. However, when James was 7, his brother died in a skating accident. To reach out to her in her depression, James "tried to gain her affection by dressing up" in his brother's clothes. One biographer noted, "The obsessive relationship that grew between mother and son was to mark the whole of his life."[2]

Some scholars have hinted that the grief—and the comforter role he filled with his mother—influenced his emotional maturity and led to a divorce years later. Laura Miller, on the eve of Peter Pan's centennial, wrote, "Barrie himself never quite grew up either."[3] What might Barrie have become had a skilled grief counselor helped free him from the burden of replacing a favored sibling?

You cannot change the past of this child.

You cannot bring back the loved one who has died.

You cannot "make it all better." Grief is something you cannot fix.

You can, however, impact the immediate present and, perhaps, the future of this child. You can make a difference in this child's experience of grief, the interpretations he or she makes of the facts and myths, and the stories he or she tells about the death.

[Name], have you ever read the story of Peter Pan? I find it interesting to know something of the life of the individual who wrote a play or story. James Barrie, like you, knew a lot about death. His brother died when James was just a boy . . .

ZOOM IN on this child

"Do you see this woman?" Jesus to Simon (Luke 7:44).

"Each of us mourned alone. Everyone in that apartment was steeped in a personal grief that did not admit the others" (Sherwin Nuland).[1]

"Do you see this child?" Jesus might well ask each one of us as our lives intersect the life of a grieving child. Charles Corr, a distinguished grief scholar, notes, "How children give or do not give vent to or share their reactions to loss depends upon the personality of the individual child, his or her ability to communicate what he or she is experiencing, and what the immediate environment (circumstances, family, culture, etc.) does or does not permit."[2]

Zoom lenses on a camera or microscope give a particular enhanced focus. In reading an article about the thousands of children in Guatemala who have lost parents to AIDS, I was overwhelmed. I cannot deal with thousands, but I can deal with one AIDS-impacted child.

If Jesus were in your community or school today, He might quiz us, "Do you see *this* child? *This* grieving child?" In His ministry Jesus responded to particular individuals. He expects those who bear His name to follow His example. We cannot reach all of the thousands of children who will be touched by death this year—but we can, one by one, reach out and comfort *a* child.

[Name], there are lots of children grieving in the world. But I am going to focus my attention on you because you deserve it. You are a special child of God, and something you teach me may help me help other grieving children. And someday, when you are grown up, you will be able to reach out to other grieving kids.

CONCLUSION: A Tale of Two Children

"There is nothing evil about the way these adults neglect the emotional needs of their children: it is just that they don't know, or have never given thought to, the emotional impact that the death of a parent or other close relative can have on a child. If they knew, they would not allow a child's fantasies to cloud reality or a child's anger to lead to destructive acts. If they knew, they would not allow a child's unresolved anger to continue into adulthood, imposing a burden of anguish for as long as a life-time" (Elizabeth Kubler-Ross).[1]

"Therefore, as we have opportunity, let us do good to all [children], especially to those who belong to the family of believers" (Gal. 6:10).

I finally located John's grave. In the snow, the flat marker was hard to find, but persistence paid off. I have long believed that markers tell stories or communicate clues that hang around in a curious mind. John, buried next to his mother, Mollie, was born in 1903 and died in 1934. As I scanned his mother's marker, a date literally jumped out at me: 1906! His mother had died when her son was three years old.

As I drove away from the Crown Hill Cemetery in Indianapolis, my mind whirled: did Mollie's death have anything to do with the life the child lived? I wondered if her death was the pivotal event that impacted a child who, as an adult, would earn the designation of Public Enemy Number One. The grave was John Dillinger's.

John Toland, in *The Dillinger Days*, described the notorious outlaw's father as "an unemotional, somber man. Though kindly, he believed any masculine display of emotion, even to a three-year-old son, was weakness."[2] Long before anyone addressed the subject of children and grief, John Wilson Dillinger "tried to instill in the youngster his own stern religious and moral principles, punishing him for the slightest misbehavior," yet at other times being overly indulgent. Johnnie had the first new bicycle on that block in Indianapolis, had money for fireworks and for candy, not only for himself but for other children too. John Wilson Dillinger, in his own pain, poured himself into running his grocery stores and making money, "sometimes locking his son in the house for safekeeping, sometimes letting him roam the neighborhood till after dark." On more that one occasion, he beat the boy with a barrel stave!

As soon as he was old enough to wait on customers, Johnnie went to work in his father's store. One day, after Johnnie slipped a pretty girl more chewing gum than she had paid for, his father snatched the gum from the stunned girl's hand, then whacked his son over the head with a large coffee can. The boy "didn't cry, just wiped the blood from his mouth and stared up at his father."[3]

Since that morning at John Dillinger's grave, I have wondered: What adults failed to reach out to that grieving child?

Several years ago, a man visiting his mother pored over old family photographs capturing him as cowboy-and-Indian, as Peter Cottontail in a first grade play, and so forth. One crumpled picture of an infant aroused his curiosity. When he turned the picture over, he found his name. Although he initially assumed that a childhood pet had gotten hold of it, he asked his mother why she had kept such a damaged photo. In answering, she told him a story that was to become important in his life.

Just after this man's first birthday, his father died of spinal lumbar polio. At age 24, he had been totally paralyzed and breathed only in an iron lung machine. Given the hysteria in those polio epidemics, few individuals visited him. But the mother faithfully visited, sitting so that he could see her in a mirror bolted to the side of the machine. That photo, his mother explained, had been crumpled so that it would fit between several knobs on the iron lung so that his father could always see his son.

I have often thought of that crumpled photo, for it is one of the few links connecting me to the stranger who was my father, a stranger who died a decade younger than I am now. Someone I have no memory of, no sensory knowledge of, spent all day every day thinking of me, devoting himself to me, loving me as he could. Perhaps, in some mysterious way, he is doing so now in another dimension. Perhaps I will have time, much time, to renew a relationship that was cruelly ended just as it had begun.[4]

No one completely gets over a significant childhood grief. Some grief waits for us to deal with it.

Two toddlers experienced significant loss. One turned out to be Public Enemy Number One, the other noted Christian author Philip Yancey. Why?

Perhaps there were no clues that tipped off caring individuals in either boy's network of adults. While I know nothing of how either boy grieved, I know how each turned out. Could John Dillinger's story have had another ending? Could Philip Yancey's story have had a different ending? Yes, Rick Warren would argue when he reminds, "You are not responsible *for* everyone in the Body of Christ, but you are responsible *to* them. God expects you to do whatever you can to help them."[5]

The grieving child that you are encountering could grow up to be either someone who will earn fame or someone who will earn shame. Make no mistake, their lives will be shaped not only by the loss they have experienced but by the compassionate care offered them not just initially but over the long term.

Such a tragedy, the death of this nine-year-old boy's mother. That October day in 1818, if you could have observed the boy whittling pegs for his mother's casket, would you have believed he had the potential for greatness? His father quickly remarried, as was custom in that day for a man with children, a compassionate widow who recognized the wound in her stepson's life. Years later, Abraham Lincoln would utter words of appreciation that have become legend: "All that I am, or hope to be, I owe to my angel mother."[6] Historian Benjamin Thomas wrote of Sarah Johnson Lincoln's influence, "Abraham adored her. Recollection of his own mother dimmed. In later years he called Sarah, who filled her role so well, 'my angel mother.'"[7]

Bad, unbelievable, unfathomable things happen to children.

Things beyond my ability to understand or explain. Things that will forever shape the future of the child. It is not so much what happens to the child but how the child, and the adults in the child's life, interpret and reinterpret the death or loss, and how those adults recognize the child's need to mourn on the child's time framework.

Caroline Kennedy, six years old, was not having a good day. Her father, the president of the United States, assassinated in Dallas, was being buried with all the pomp and ceremony a grieving nation could muster. She rode with her brother John and her nanny, Maude Shaw, in the backseat of a limousine slowly making it's way toward St. Matthew's Cathedral. Her mother and uncles Robert and Ted—and numerous world leaders—were walking in front of the limousine. Caroline looked out the window and recognized Robert Foster, a Secret Service agent. She rolled down the window and stuck out her hand and the agent took it and held it tightly all the way to the church. Agent Foster later said that it was all he could do to keep from bursting into tears.[8]

That day a Secret Service agent made a difference for a six-year-old girl.

You do not have to be a Secret Service agent to make a difference. The child does not have to be the daughter of a president. You simply have to be willing to be interrupted for the sake of a grieving child. You can make a difference in a child's integration of the loss and how that initial loss will impact other losses. You simply have to have eyes open to small hands sticking out of limousine windows.

I close this book with an old chorus, sung in my childhood, and occasionally since, substituting one word:

> Lord, lay some child upon my heart
> And love that child through me.
> And may I always do my part
> To love that child for Thee.

There was nothing to indicate that the seven-year-old in Midland, Texas, would grow up to be president. But the death of his four-year-old sister and the changes in his family were to have a lasting impact. George W. Bush wrote, "I guess I learned at an early age never to take life for granted. But rather than making me fearful, the close reach of death made me determined, determined to enjoy whatever life might bring, to live each day to the fullest."[9]

It all comes down to a string of words: Grieving children should be seen and heard!

APPENDICES

APPENDIX A: Guidelines for Professional Evaluation of Grieving Children

William Worden, distinguished psychologist and author of *When Children Grieve*, identifies the following "red-flag behaviors" by a child that should be evaluated by a professional counselor. Clearly, many initial disturbing behaviors will be short-lived and will self-limit. "The focus," in Worden's judgment, "should not be on the presence of a symptom or behavior but on the duration."

1. Persistent difficulty talking about the dead parent. Remember that some children will have difficulty talking about the death.
2. Aggressive behavior that persists or takes the form of property destruction.
3. Persistent anxiety: the child clings to the surviving parent or exhibits phobic behavior about going to school.
4. Persistent psychosomatic problems such as stomachaches and headaches or prolonged bodily distress.
5. Persistent sleeping disorders for a number of months or persisting nightmares.
6. Persistent changes in eating behaviors (not eating or aggressively overeating).
7. Persistent marked social withdrawal—the child wants to be alone.
8. Persistent school social difficulties or serious academic reversal.
9. Persistent self-blame or guilt or a sense of unworthiness.
10. Self-destructive behaviors or the expression of a desire to die. "Although this behavior is less common, it must be taken seriously. Some children miss their dead parent so much that they express a desire to die and rejoin the lost parent."[1]

Even clinicians have difficulty, with certain grieving children, ascertaining "when behavior is a normal response to loss and when it becomes pathological."[2] The goal is to notice the grieving child. Some persistent behaviors are pleas for recognition: *Would someone recognize that I am grieving too?* In most cases, the child will not require long-term counseling care.

APPENDIX B: Child's Permission to Grieve Slip

PERMISSION TO MOURN:

---

as a child of God

you are hereby entitled to tell people about

your loss, mourn openly, to share stories

about the loss, and to ask for help, in your

own way and time, without apology or

embarrassment.

Tears, memories, silence, uncertainty, and

strong emotions are OK. You always

deserve kindness, compassion, and love.

This certificate has no expiration date.

APPENDIX C: Remarkable Resources for Grieving Children

Johnson, Joy, and Earl Grollman. *A Child's Book About Burial and Cremation*. Omaha: Centering Corporation, 2001. Thirteen pages of child-friendly explanations on burial, cemeteries and cremation.

———. *A Child's Book About Death*. Omaha: Centering Corporation, 2001. Thirteen pages of child-friendly materials. Excellent ideas for children. Includes space for children to write and draw.

———. *A Child's Book About Funerals and Rituals*. Omaha: Centering Corporation, 2001. A wonderful 18-page resource that will prepare children for the funeral and burial rituals. Also contains space for the child's questions and recollections.

Johnson, Joy, and Marvin Johnson. *Tell Me Papa: Answers to Questions Children Ask About Death and Dying*. Omaha: Centering Corporation, 1978. Grandparents may not be the ones to break the news of a death, but they are natural comforters and listeners. This book addresses the incredible questions that children have about death, dying, and grieving.

Mellonie, Bryan, and Robert Ingpen. *Lifetimes: The Beautiful Way to Explain Death to Children*. New York: Bantam, 1983. *Lifetimes* is a moving book for explaining death to children of all ages. Adults will also find comfort in the sensitive text and beautiful drawings. The book communicates that dying is a part of living. This book addresses long and short lifetimes.

Scrivani, Mark. *I Heard Your Daddy Died*. Omaha: Centering Corporation, 1996. This book is a friend to the adult who wants to help grieving children ages 6 to 9. These practical questions that initiate conversations and provocative drawings by children create a must resource on your shelf. [See also *I Heard Your Mommy Died* by the same author.]

———. *I Heard Your Mommy Died*. Omaha: Centering Corporation, 1996. Wonderful resource for children 6 to 9 that gives permission to be a child and permission to grieve. Drawings by children in the book are excellent.

Traisman, Enid Samuel. *Remember: A Child Remembers*. Omaha: Centering Corporation, 1994. This write-in memory book for grieving children is a resource children will treasure. Gives the child space to describe the deceased through prodding clues like: your favorite color, hobby, pet, places. You were good at . . . A list of memories I will want to always remember as well as a space to write a good-bye letter.

Wolfelt, Alan D. *Healing Your Grieving Heart for Kids: 100 Practical Ideas*. Ft. Collins, Colo.: Companion Books, 2001. In this resource designed for readers 6 to 12 years old who are grieving, Wolfelt gives 100 practical ideas that affirm and nurture the grieving child, such as "don't let anybody take your grief away from you, list the things that are still good about life, don't be scared by griefbursts." Order the companion book for adults, *Healing a Child's Grieving Heart.*

APPENDIX D: Resources That Will Help You Help Grieving Children

These resources are offered with confidence. Admittedly, not every book reflects a distinctly "Christian" perspective. However, these resources will provide ideas you can adapt to make a difference in a grieving child's life. Urge that these books be in your church library and on the bookshelf of professionals who work with children.

Fitzgerald, Helen. *The Grieving Child: A Parent's Guide.* New York: Fireside, 1992. Explaining death is one of the most difficult tasks a loving adult can face. Arranged by topics, you will find materials you can put your eyes on immediately.

Huntley, Theresa M. *Helping Children Grieve: When Someone They Love Dies.* Rev. ed. Minneapolis: Augsburg, 2002. Huntley shows how children of various ages understand and can begin to comprehend death. It is not a question of if death touches the life of a child you love but when and how you will help or hinder that child.

———. *When Your Child Loses a Loved One.* Minneapolis: Augsburg, 2001. What comforts an adult griever may confuse or even distress a child. In this short, 56-page book you will find help in addressing some of life's toughest questions.

Johnson, Joy. *Keys to Helping Children Deal with Death and Grief.* New York: Barron's, 1999. An outstanding book to help parents and careers explain the facts and feelings of death in ways that are understandable to children. The advice is in short, readable chapters.

Kroen, William C. *Helping Children Cope with the Loss of a Loved One: A Guide for Grown-Ups.* Minneapolis: Free Spirit, 1996. In clear, concise language, Kroen, a licensed psychotherapist for children in crisis, offers advice for any adult who is helping a child cope with the death of a loved one.

Silverman, Phyllis Rolfe. *Never Too Young to Know: Death in Children's Lives.* New York: Oxford, 2000. For readers who want a scholarly approach, this definitive resource offers a practical look and theoretical framework for discovering how children grieve in today's world.

Wolfelt, Alan D. *Healing a Child's Grieving Heart: 100 Practical Ideas for Families, Friends and Caregivers.* Fort Collins, Colo.: Companion Books, 2001. How do you help a grieving child? This handy guide offers 100 practical, will-work ideas for helping children do grief work. A concise, easy-to-use resource.

Wright, Norm. *It's Okay to Cry.* Colorado Springs: WaterBrook, 2004. With 30 years of counseling experience in the Christian community, Norm Wright is a trusted friend to many parents. Through anecdotes and discussion questions, Wright offers practical advice on grief issues.

APPENDIX E: A Vocabulary for Talking About Death with Children

"When I use a word, it means just what I choose to mean— neither more or less." Alice protests, "The question is whether you can make words mean so many different things" (Humpty Dumpty in Carroll).[1]

Grieving individuals need words to express their loss; care-givers need words to comfort. Alice raises a good point because words mean different things to different hearers. The child may overhear certain words and confuse them with other meanings. Consider, in a child's world, the similarity, at least in sound, between *mourning* and *morning*. Or *trust* as a way of setting aside money for future use but also a relationship between two people.

These child-friendly definitions will help you communicate. The written definition is a starting point. You may want to expand it or use it in a sentence. Or first ask the child what he or she thinks the word means. Write the word on one side of an index card and the definition on the other. The child can start the conversation by drawing a word.

Accidental death: An unplanned death as a result of an automobile wreck or fall. The doctors and nurses could not keep the body working because of the injuries.

Autopsy: An operation done by a doctor called a pathologist to look inside the body after death to find out why the person died. In most cases, an autopsy helps doctors and families understand why a person died and helps the police catch a criminal who caused the death.

Burial: Placing the corpse in a casket or the cremated remains in an urn, in the ground. Below ground, the burial space is called a grave; above ground, the space in a mausoleum or columbarium is called a niche.

Casket: *A wood or metal box in which the dead person is buried.* Some people call the container a *coffin.* Actually, a coffin is body-shaped and does not have handles, while a casket is a long rectangle box. Caskets come in different sizes and colors.

Cemetery: *A place for burying dead human bodies or cremated remains.* Cemeteries at a church are called graveyards. Some cemeteries are called *memorial parks or gardens.*

Closed casket: Some people do not want family and friends to view the body after death, so they request the casket lid be kept closed. Sometimes, in a wreck, explosion, war, terrorism, or as a result of a long illness, the body is so damaged that it is better if the casket is kept closed.

Columbarium: A special room where cremated remains are kept.

Committal: The burial service is called the committal because the family and friends commit the soul to God's care and the body to the earth. Often a minister reads scriptures like the 23rd psalm and prays. Some families or family members leave immediately; others watch the casket lowered into the grave.

Condolences: Special words used to describe how sorry we are that someone died.

Corpse: A human or animal body that is dead.

Cremation: The process of turning the body into a fine ash called *cremated remains,* which can be stored in an urn, scattered, or buried.

Cremated remains: The ash that is left after cremation. Some people call these *cremains* and some call them *ashes.*

Dead: *When an individual's body or brain stops working,* the body cannot feel, see, hear, hurt, smell, eat, or breathe, sing, cry, go to the bathroom, or laugh anymore. The person cannot come back to life although you may have seen that happen in movies or cartoons. Some individuals prefer to say that the individual has "passed" or "passed away" or "has gone to be with the Lord."

Death certificate: A legal document that reports when, where, and how the individual died. It is official proof for courts, banks, and insurance companies that the individual died.

Embalm: *A procedure that prepares the body for viewing and burial.* The corpse is washed, the hair shampooed, then dressed. Light makeup is put on the face. The Bible says that when Jesus died, women friends prepared and "anointed" the body for burial.

Estate: What a person owned at the time of death including money, cars, houses, boats, stocks, property, businesses, farms, or animals. You may overhear someone say, "We have to settle *the estate.*" That is an orderly way to divide the goods, property, and money that belonged to the individual who died.

Estate sale: A special sale, like a yard or garage sale, often at the deceased's home, to sell items that the family does not want to keep.

Family car: A special car or limousine in which family members ride together to the funeral, to the church, or to the cemetery. Some families feel more comfortable riding in their own car.

Funeral: At this special service families, friends and neighbors say goodbye, remember the person who died and comfort the family. Some families want the funeral to be like a church service (only no offering or Communion is taken). The funeral either takes place at the church or at the funeral home.

Funeral director: *A person who cares for the body before burial and helps the family with details of the funeral.* In some communities, this caring individual is called an *undertaker* or *mortician.* Like physicians, nurses, and attorneys, the funeral director has to go to school to learn how to help grieving people.

Funeral home: *A special building where bodies are cared for until burial.* Many visitations and funerals take place there. One reason it is called a funeral home is that it is designed to look like a living room and sometimes a funeral director's family lives upstairs.

Funeral procession: The ride from the church or funeral home to the cemetery. In ancient times people carried torches in the procession to the grave so that is why cars in the procession have the lights on.

Grave: *The place where the casket or urn will be buried.*

Grief: *The thoughts and feelings (like anger or sadness) individuls have after someone's death.* Grief can be different for different people; your dad might cry and your mom may not cry at all.

Headstone: *A marker made of marble or granite or metal that identifies the grave.* Some people call markers headstones because they are at the head of the grave. Other people call them *tombstones* or *monuments.* The marker tells when the person lived and died.

Hearse: *A special car used to take the casket.* A hearse was once an elegant wagon pulled by special horses.

Heaven: A wonderful place God has prepared for everyone who loves Him. It is a beautiful place where, according to one child, "nothing bad ever happens." No one ever gets sick or hurt in heaven. Another child said, "And you get to see Jesus anytime you want to." The Bible says that no one can even imagine how wonderful heaven is.

Homicide: *To deliberately kill a human being. Some people call this murder.*

Loved one: *A term of affection for a person who has died.* Some people do not like to say *the deceased,* so instead they focus on the love you had for the individual.

Mausoleum: *A special building in cemeteries where human bodies or cremated remains are buried above ground.* Some family members do not want their loved ones buried in the ground.

Memorial service: *A service to honor the deceased only there is no casket or corpse present.* If the individual has been cremated, the urn containing the cremated remains may be present. Sometimes, a memorial service takes place days or weeks after the death.

Memories: The things you remember about a person, like how much they loved pizza or soccer games or cats or disliked liver.

Miscarriage: *Sometimes before a baby is born, the baby dies inside its mother.* Doctors and moms and dads and grandparents do not always know why the baby died, but it's nobody's fault.

Mourning: *The outward ways humans show grief, like crying or sobbing or being sad.*

Mystery: *Something that cannot be explained or understood.* It is common when a child or young adult or parent dies for people to ask *why*. Sometimes, there are no good reasons for a death.

Obituary: *A special newspaper article about the deceased.* In some communities these are called *death notices*. Obituaries help friends know when to come to the funeral home or to the funeral. Some obituaries have pictures.

Organ donor: Organs are body parts that have special functions: the heart, for example, pumps the blood; the kidneys keep the blood clean; the brain tells the heart to pump the blood. A person can decide that certain body organs are to be given to someone who needs the body part. Some families, after the death, agree to donate body parts to another sick individual. Although you are sad that your loved one died, you can be glad that in a sense he or she "lives on" in giving health to another person.

Pallbearer: Individuals who carry the casket at the funeral and committal. Individuals who carry an urn are called urnbearers.

Plot: The special space at the cemetery where the body will be buried. Some families buy several plots so that family members can be buried close to one another.

Probate: A special court that makes certain that all the deceased's bills have been paid and that the deceased's wishes in the will have been followed.

Suicide: *When a person deliberately ends his or her own life.* Sometimes a person is so really sad that he or she does not want to live anymore.

Sudden infant death syndrome: *Sometimes babies stop breathing while sleeping and die.* It does not happen because of anything anybody did or did not do.

Trust: A legal document that allows people to leave money to be used in the future for a certain purpose. For example, your grandmother might leave money in a trust to pay for your college education.

Urn: *A metal, glass, or stone container in which cremated remains are kept.*

Vault: A *box* of concrete or steel that protects the casket in the ground. The casket fits inside the vault. Some call spaces in a mausoleum a vault.

Viewing: *A time for family and friends, if they wish, to view the body and tell family members how sorry they are. Individual often share memories and stories about the deceased.*

Widow: *Spouse of a man who has died.*

Widower: *Spouse of a woman who has died.*

Will: *A legal document that explains how the dead person wanted his or her possessions distributed.* "After I die, I want money to go to . . ." An *executor* —chosen by the deceased—is the individual who makes sure that the wishes are followed.

Sources consulted:

Johnson, Joy. *Keys to Helping Children Deal with Death and Grief.* Naupphaufe, N.Y.: Barron's Educational Services, 1999, 163-67.

Wolfelt, Alan D. *The Journey Through Grief: Reflections on Healing.* Fort Collins, Colo.: Companion Press, 1997, 141-43.

Wolfelt, Alan D. "Clientcare," *The Director* (1994, June), 51-52.

Special thanks to Nancy Keller, Elliott and Anna Keller, Marilyn Mokhtarian, Arvil Pennington, Dr. Sally Higgins, and Professor Valerie Bosco of the University of San Francisco for their suggestions in formulating these definitions.

APPENDIX F: Recommended Children's Books with Grief Themes

It can take years for a child and adult to talk through all there is to say about a death. These recommended books can be read *with* a child, again and again. Before you select a book, read through the book first and familiarize yourself with its contents before you read it with the child. What questions might the book raise?

Alexander, Sue. *Nadia the Willful*. New York: Pantheon Books, 1983. Nadia's brother, Hamed, perishes in a desert storm. Her father orders that his name never be mentioned again in the oasis. Nadia challenges that edict. *Implications for grievers:* Sometimes a griever has to challenge the "forget and move on" mentality. (Although this book is currently out-of-print, look for it. It is well worth the search.)

Bostrom, Kathleen Long. *Papa's Gift: An Inspirational Story of Love and Loss*. Grand Rapids: Zonderkidz, 2002. Clara cannot understand why God let her grandfather die. Why didn't God answer her prayer? Through a special gift from her grandfather she begins to understand how she can keep her grandfather in her heart.

Brown, Laurie Krasny, and Marc Brown. *When Dinosaurs Die: A Guide to Understanding Death*. Boston: Little, Brown and Company, 1996. The authors cleverly use dinosaurs to tell the story of life and death. Children find permission to experience a wide range of emotions toward death and the individual(s) who died. The book also addresses fears that children may develop following the death of a loved one. *Implications for grievers:* This practical resource honestly deals with death and offers an excellent section on ways to remember and has a comprehensive, child-friendly vocabulary of words associated with death.

Coville, Bruce. *My Grandfather's House*. New York: BridgeWater Books, 1996. What do children experience when they go to a grandparent's house or apartment but learn, "Grandpa doesn't live here anymore?" The questions that naturally arise can be opportunities for learning. The child in the story concludes, "Someday I will know more. But that's enough for now."

Evans, Richard Paul, and Jonathan Linton. *The Dance*. [New York: Simon and Schuster Books for Young Readers, 1999. Follow the role of dancing in a young girl's life. At every stage her father is present, encouraging her. Then, in her father's final illness, the young woman is asked to come home to dance one last time. She must struggle with how she will remember. *Implications for grievers:* The adult who has been a significant encourager remains in our lives through memory. We do not

147

have to forget those we love. The story illustrates what Phyllis Silverman calls "continuing bonds."

Fox, Mem. *Wilfrid Gordon McDonald Partridge*. La Jolla, Calif.: Kane/Miller, 1985. A six-year-old's question, "What's a memory?" sparks great interaction in a nursing home as the boy asks residents to explain memory. "Something that makes you feel warm." "Something from long ago." "Something that makes you cry." "Something that makes you laugh." "Something as precious as gold." *Implications for grievers:* What stimulates memories for you? Introduces the variety of memory initiators. This book has wonderful pictures and will be valued by the child griever (and by adults too).

Howe, James, and David Rose. *There's a Monster Under My Bed*. New York: Alladin, 1986. Simon is sure that there are monsters under his bed in the night—he can even hear them breathing! Grief can be the unspoken "monster" that menaces a child's sense of safety and security. *Implications for grievers:* In the presence of "monsters under our beds," grievers need company.

Lobel, Arnold. *Frog and Toad Together*. New York: Harper and Row, 1971. One of the gifts of a friend is his or her presence. The essay "Alone" describes the ability of two close friends "to sit alone, together" sometimes without talking. *Implications for grievers:* We do not have to know what to say—we simply show up.

Munsch, Robert. *Love You Forever*. Willowdale, Ontario: Firefly Books, Portunus Publishing, 1986. A mother's promise, "Love you forever, like you for always . . ." is promised and honored through the stages of development of a boy's life. *Implications for grievers:* The book helps grievers of all ages realize that others know that love lasts longer than grief and gives permission to love forever.

Root, Phyllis. *The Name Quilt*. New York: Farrar, Straus and Giroux, 2003. The nights Sadie spends at Grandma's house she sleeps under the name quilt. The quilt has the names of all the family members, and as Sadie learns, each name and piece of fabric is linked to a story. When a storm blows the quilt off the clothesline, Sadie is sad until she discovers that her grandmother keeps "all the names and all of those stories right here inside me." *Implications for grievers:* The book helps grieving children find ways to remember their loved one and to know that even if the object is lost, the memory remains.

Scrivani, Mark. *I Heard Your Daddy Died*. Omaha: Centering Corporation, 1996. What do you say to a grieving child after, "I heard your daddy died"? Scrivani offers wise guidance. The book shows great sensitivity and will be a valued resource for the care-er. *Implications for grievers:* The book gives valuable ways to initiate conversations with grieving children. [See also *I Heard Your Mommy Died* by the same author.]

Rylant, Cynthia. *Cat Heaven*. New York: Scholastic, 1997. If dogs go to heaven, what about cats? "If you have ever been lucky enough to have a special cat in your life, then you well know there is someplace called Cat Heaven!" *Implications for grievers:* The book helps adults realize that others "know" grief too and that we can all learn from one another.

———. *Dog Heaven*. New York: Scholastic, 1995. Do dogs go to heaven when they die? Rylant says yes. "When a dog arrives in heaven, he just runs." Rylant adds, "They will be there when old friends show up. They will be there at the door." *Implications for grievers:* The book helps grievers realize that grief for pets is acceptable.

Shulevitz, Uri. *The Treasure*. New York: Sunburst/Farrar, Straus and Giroux, 1978. Isaac has a dream about treasure buried in a distant city. A guard has a dream about treasure buried under a fellow named Isaac's stove. The moral: Sometimes one must travel far to discover what is near. *Implications for grievers*: Bereavement is a journey. And, at the end, we discover that some of the most valued resources were near us, all the time.

Simon, Norma. *The Saddest Time*. Morton Grove, Ill.: Albert Whitman and Company, 1986. When someone dies, it is natural to feel sad. Simon offers children three scenarios: the death of a young uncle, the death of a schoolmate, and the death of a grandmother. The book helps children balance sadness with new beginnings.

Thomas, Jane Resh. *Saying Good-bye to Grandma*. New York: Clarion, 1988. Clara, on the long ride to her grandmother's house, is wondering what the funeral will be like. Through a series of experiences, she comes to develop an understanding of death and of funeral rituals.

NOTES

Introduction

1. Helen Fitzgerald, *The Grieving Child: A Parent's Guide* (New York: Fireside, 1992), 42.

2. Arthur Ashe and Alexander McNab, *Arthur Ashe on Tennis: Strokes, Strategies, Traditions, Players, Psychology, and Wisdom* (New York: Knopf, 1995), 50.

3. Ibid.

4. Andrew Lester, ed., *Ministry with Children in Crisis* (Philadelphia: Westminster Press, 1987), 10. In Andrew D. Lester, ed., *When Children Suffer: A Sourcebook for Ministry with Children in Crisis*, 9-15.

AUDIT your own grief experience

1. William C. Kroen, *Helping Children Cope with the Loss of a Loved One: A Guide for Grownups* (Minneapolis: Free Spirit Press, 1996), 70.

2. Phyllis Rolfe Silverman, *Never Too Young to Know: Death in Children's Lives* (New York: Oxford University Press, 2000), 4.

3. Priscilla LeMone and Karen Burke, eds., *Medical-Surgical Nursing: Critical Thinking in Client Care*, 3rd ed. (Upper Saddle River, N.J.: Pearson/Prentice-Hall, 2004), 319.

4. Dorothy Schneider and Carl J. Schneider, *First Ladies: A Biographical Dictionary* (New York: Checkmark Books, 2001), 281.

5. Jan Jarboe Russell, *Lady Bird: A Biography of Mrs. Johnson* (New York: Scribner, 1999), 54.

6. Ibid.

7. Ibid., 55.

8. Ibid.

9. Barbara Bush, *Barbara Bush: A Memoir* (New York: Charles Scribner's Sons, 1994), 46.

10. George W. Bush, *A Charge to Keep I Have* (New York: William Morrow, 1999), 14.

11. Elizabeth Arias, Marian F. MacDorman, Donna M. Strobino, and Bernard Guyer, "Annual Survey of Vital Statistics—2002," *Pediatrics* 112(8), 1225.

12. Ron Oliver, Personal conversation (December 17, 2003).

13. Dexter King with Ralph Wiley, *Growing Up King: An Intimate Memoir* (New York: Warner, 2003), 75.

14. Aaron Latham, "How George W. Found God," *George* (September 2000), 80.

15. Ibid., 81.

16. Ibid.

17. Ibid.

18. Fitzgerald, *Grieving Child*, 42.

19. John Kennedy, *The Uncommon Wisdom of JFK*. Ed. Bill Adler and Tom Folsom (New York: Rugged Land, 2003), 113.

RECOGNIZING individuality

1. Christopher Andersen, *Sweet Caroline: Last Child of Camelot* (New York: William Morrow, 2003), 81.

2. Norman H. Wright, *It's Okay to Cry: A Parent's Guide to Helping Children Through the Losses of Life* (Colorado Springs, Colo.: WaterBrook, 2004), 64 (in manuscript format).

3. Theresa Huntley, *When Your Child Loses a Loved One* (Minneapolis: Augsburg, 2001), 34-35.

4. Linda Goldman, *A Look at Children's Grief* (module 1: Children's Loss and Grief) [CD] (Hartford, Conn.: Association for Death Education and Counseling, 2001).

5. Andersen, *Sweet Caroline*, 90.

6. Christopher Andersen, *The Day John Died* (New York: William Morrow, 2000), 73.

7. Joy Johnson, *Keys to Helping Children Deal with Death and Grief* (New York: Barron's, 1999), 18-19.

8. Ibid., 18.

9. Fitzgerald, The *Grieving Child*, 55.

10. Madeleine Albright with Bill Woodward, *Madame Secretary: A Memoir* (New York: Miramax Books, 2003), 11.

11. Ibid., 241.

12. Ibid.

13. Andersen, *The Day John Died*, 91.

14. Alan D. Wolfelt, *Healing a Child's Grieving Heart: 100 Practical Ideas* (Fort Collins, Colo.: Companion Press, 2001), 21.

15. Edward Klein, *Just Jackie: Her Private Years* (New York: Ballantine, 1998).

16. Hendrik Booraem, *Young Hickory: The Making of Andrew Jackson* (Dallas: Taylor Trade Publishing, 2001), 110-11.

17. Mary Jordan, "Always a Coffin Waiting" at AIDS Orphans Hospice, *San Francisco Chronicle* (November 28, 2003), C2.

18. Sherwin Nuland, *How We Die: Reflections on Life's Final Chapter* (New York: Knopf, 1994), xviii.

19. George H. Nash, *The Life of Herbert Hoover: The Engineer, 1874-1914* (New York: W. W. Norton, 1983), 8-12.

20. B. Krietemeyer and S. P. Heiney, "Storytelling as a Therapeutic Technique in Group for School-age Oncology Patients," *Children's Health Care* 21 (1992), 14-20.

21. Wright, *It's Okay to Cry*, 78 (in manuscript format).

22. Peter A. Selwyn, *Surviving the Fall: The Personal Journey of an AIDS Doctor* (New Haven, Conn.: Yale University Press, 1998), 113.

23. Ibid., 114.

24. Ibid., 107.

25. Ibid., 115.

26. Ibid., 124.

27. Ibid., 107.

28. Katherine Ashenburg, *The Mourner's Dance: What We Do When People Die* (New York: North Point Press, 2003), 3.

29. Andersen, *Sweet Caroline*, 86-87.

30. Ibid., 104.

ASK: How do I help *this* child?
1. Kroen, *Helping Children Cope*, 37.

AFFIRM this child
1. Bush, *A Charge to Keep*, 15.
2. Schneider and Schneider, *First Ladies*, 281.

AVOID overloading the child with too many details
1. Maureen Rank, *Free to Grieve: Healing and Encouragement for Those Who Have Experienced the Physical, Mental, and Emotional Trauma of Miscarriage and Stillbirth* (Minneapolis: Bethany House, 1985), 127.

ASSESS: To whom is this child listening?
1. Fitzgerald, *Grieving Child*, 101.
2. Andersen, *Sweet Caroline*, 105.
3. Mariana Caplan, *When Holidays Are Hell! A Guide to Surviving Family Gatherings* (Prescott, Ariz.: Hohm Press, 1997), 89.
4. Silverman, *Never Too Young to Know*, 9.
5. Wolfelt, *Healing a Child's Grieving Heart*, 7.

ADVOCATE for this child and for grieving children
1. Dick Gilbert, cited in Johnson, *Keys to Helping Children Deal with Death and Grief*, 110.
2. Phyllis R. Silverman, John Baker, Cheryl-Anne Cait, and Kathryn Boerner, "The Effects of Negative Legacies on the Adjustment of Parentally Bereaved Children and Adolescents," *Omega* 46(4) (2002-3), 349.
3. Goldman, *A Look at Children's Grief.*

ANTICIPATE tough special days on the child's calendar
1. Fitzgerald, *Grieving Child*, 108.

ANSWER honestly and accurately
1. Sandi Kahn Shelton, "Word to the Whys," *U.S. Airways Attache* (February 2001), 34.
2. Kathryn N. Chapman, "What Children Need from Significant Adults," in Andrew D. Lester, ed., *When Children Suffer: A Sourcebook for Ministry with Children in Crisis* (Philadelphia: Westminster Press, 1987), 53.
3. Goldman, *A Look at Children's Grief.*
4. Victoria Alexander, *Words I Never Thought to Speak: Stories of Life in the Wake of Suicide* (New York: Lexington Books, 1991), x.
5. Chapman, "What Children Need," 55.
6. Kroen, *Helping Children Cope*, 8.
7. Robert A. Neimeyer, *Lessons of Loss: A Guide to Coping* (New York: McGraw-Hill/Primis Custom Publishing, 1998), 42.
8. Goldman, *A Look at Children's Grief.*

ATTEND rituals
1. Laurie Krasny Brown and Marc Brown, *When Dinosaurs Die: A Guide to Understanding Death* (Boston: Little, Brown, 1996), 25.

AVOID euphemisms
1. Fitzgerald, *The Grieving Children*, 44.

BE there for the child!

1. Barbara Kozier, Glenora Erb, Audrey Jean Berman, and Karen Burke, eds., *Fundamentals of Nursing: Concepts, Process, and Practice*, 6th ed. (Upper Saddle River, N.J.: Prentice Hall Health, 2000), 976.

2. Ibid., 105.

3. Ibid., 106.

4. Dietrich Bonhoeffer, *Life Together*. Trans. John W. Doberstein (New York: Harper and Row, 1954), 99.

BE real!

1. Silverman, *Never Too Young to Know*, 246.

CELEBRATE heaven

1. Dean in Timothy Freke, ed., *Children's Visions of Heaven and Hell: Innocent Observations of the Aftermath* (Liguori, Mo.: Triumph Books, 1997), 16.

2. Ethel Young in Mary Ellen Berry and Carmen Renee Berry, *Reawakening to Life: Renewal After a Husband's Death* (New York: Crossroad Carlisle, 2002), 87-88.

3. Freke, *Heaven*, 26.

4. Elizabeth Liggett Reed, *Helping Children with the Mystery of Death* (Nashville: Abingdon, 1970), 26.

5. Ron Oliver, "Heaven Is the Place Where Nothing Ever Goes Wrong," *The Journal of Pastoral Care* 55(2) (2001), 203.

6. Andersen, *Sweet Caroline*, 89.

7. Wolfelt, *Healing a Child's Grieving Heart*, 27.

CHILD-SIZE the holidays

1. Caplan, *When Holidays Are Hell*, 79.

CREATE a collage

1. Huntley, *When Your Child Loses a Loved One*, 49.

COMMEMORATE the life

1. Goldman, *A Look at Children's Grief*.

DE-FAULT the child

1. Rank, *Free to Grieve*, 128.

2. Jeanne Phillips, "Dear Abby: Children Need to Know Truth About Dying Parents," *Kansas City Star* (October 23, 2003), F4.

3. James Robert Parish, *Rosie: Rosie O'Donnell's Biography* (New York: Carroll and Graf, 1997), 5.

4. Barbara Bush, *Reflections: Life After the White House* (New York: Lisa Drew/Scribner, 2003), 204.

DRAW and COLOR

1. Kroen, *Helping Children Cope*, 55.

2. Fern Reiss, *Terrorism and Kids: Comforting Your Child* (Boston: Peanut Butter and Jelly Press, 2001), 153.

3. J. William Worden, *Children and Grief: When a Parent Dies* (New York: Guilford, 1996), 162.

DO NOT DISTRACT this child from grief
   1. Rank, *Free to Grieve*, 129.

ENCOURAGE keeping routines
   1. Kroen, *Helping Children Cope*, 86-87.

FINANCE counseling
   1. Edith Roosevelt cited in Conrad Black, *Franklin Delano Roosevelt: Champion of Freedom* (New York: Public Affairs, 2003), 37.
   2. Wolfelt, *Healing a Child's Grieving Heart*, intro.
   3. Blanche Wiesen Cook, *Eleanor Roosevelt*, Vol. 1: 1884-1933 (New York: Viking, 1992), 79.
   4. Ibid., 79-80.
   5. David Roosevelt, *Grandmere: A Personal History of Eleanor Roosevelt* (New York: Warner Books, 2002), 60.
   6. Black, *Roosevelt: Champion of Freedom*, 37.
   7. Worden, *Children and Grief*, 160-61.
   8. Ibid., 153-54.
   9. U.S. Bureau of the Census, "Low Income Uninsured Children by State" (2004). Http://www.census.govc/hhes/hlthins/liuc02.html.
   10. Worden, *Children and Grief*, 151.
   11. Ibid., 152.
   12. Christine Dugas, "Prepaid Funeral Can Have Pitfalls: Check All Factors Before Putting Funds into Final Resting Place," *USA Today* (September 26, 2003), 3B.
   13. Tony Pugh, "Number of uninsured rose dramatically last year, figures show" (Published by Knight-Ridder, September 30, 2003). Http://www.common dreams.org/cgi-bin/print.cgi?file=headlines03/0930-0l.htm.
   14. Earl A. Grollman, "Grieving Children: Can We Answer Their Questions?" in Kenneth J. Doka, ed., *Children Mourning, Mourning Children* (Washington Hospice Foundation of America, 1995), 26.

FUND some special events
   1. Hillary Rodham Clinton, "It Takes a Village," *Newsweek* (January 15, 1996), 31.

GIVE the child permission to grieve
   1. Lady Bird Johnson cited in Russell, *Lady Bird*, 53.
   2. Rank, *Free to Grieve*, 128.

GUARD confidences shared by a child
   1. Roosevelt, *Grandmere*, 59.

GO to the cemetery or scattering area
   1. Sherwin B. Nuland, *Lost in America: A Journey with My Father* (New York: Alfred N. Knopf, 2003), n.p.
   2. Henri Nouwen, "A Picnic on a Tombstone and Other Reflections," *New Oxford Review* (March 1994), 94-95.
   3. Todd Little, Personal correspondence (December 19, 2003).

GIVE this grieving child permission to have fun
   1. Mark Scrivani, *I Heard Your Daddy Died* (Omaha: The Centering Corporation, 1996), n.p.

2. Stuart Brown cited in Ken McAlpine (2003, December). The Young and the Restless: Today's kids are taught that multitasking is where it's at. We could all be very wrong. *American Way*, 55.

HELP create a child-focused obituary

1. Suzy Yehl Marta, *Healing the Hurt, Restoring the Hope* (Philadelphia: Rodale Press, 2003), 88.

HONOR the child's anger

1. Cheryl Ross Staats, Katherine A. Pollard, Catherine E. Brown, "End-of-Life Care," in Sharon Mantik Lewis, Margaret McLean Heitkemper, and Shannon Ruff Dirksen, eds. *Medical-Surgical Nursing: Assessment and Management of Clinical Problems*, 6th ed. (St. Louis: Mosby, 2004), 169.

INCLUDE children in rituals of grieving

1. Wright, *It's Okay to Cry*, 78 (in manuscript format).

2. Goldman, *A Look at Children's Grief*.

JOURNAL your feelings, questions, anxieties

1. Susan A. Muto, *Pathways of Spiritual Living* (Garden City, N.J.: Doubleday, 1984), 94-95.

2. Richard Foster, *Freedom of Simplicity* (San Francisco: Harper and Row, 1978), 109.

KNOW warning signals

1. Kroen, *Helping Children Cope*, 70.

2. Ibid., 74.

3. Ibid., 70.

LET this child still be a child

1. Susan E. Richardson, *Holidays and Holy Days: Origins, Customs, and Insights on Celebrations Through the Year* (Ann Arbor, Mich.: Servant Publications, 2001), 161.

2. Helen Bryan, *Martha Washington: First Lady of Liberty* (New York: John Wiley and Sons, 2002), 73.

LINGER

1. Chapman, "What Children Need," 43.

2. Robert Munsch, *Where Is Gah-Ning?* (Toronto: Annick, 1994), n.p.

LOBBY for stability

1. Kroen, *Helping Children Cope*, 87.

LET a child's curiosity guide the discussion

1. Eda LeShan, *Learning to Say Good-bye: When a Parent Dies* (New York: Macmillian, 1976), 14.

2. Andersen, *Sweet Caroline*, 91.

MAKE a memory box

1. Bill Dodds, *Your Grieving Child: Answers to Questions on Death and Dying* (Huntington, Ind.: Our Sunday Visitor, 2002), 61.

MAKE lists

1. Russell Ash, *Fascinating Book of 1001 Lists* (New York: D.K. Publishing, 1999), 6.

2. Worden, *Children and Grief*, 165.

NIP any criticism of the child or the family's grief

1. Andrew Puckett Jr. "The Bereaved Child," in Andrew D. Lester, ed., *When Children Suffer: A Sourcebook for Ministry with Children in Crisis* (Philadelphia: Westminster Press, 1987), 93.

2. James A. Fogarty, *The Magical Thoughts of Children* (Amityville, N.Y.: Baywood, 2000), 168-69.

3. Worden, *Children and Grief*, 154.

NOTICE behavioral changes

1. Judith Allen Shelly and Sharon Fish, e-mail (January 23, 2004).

2. Alan D. Wolfelt, *A Child's View of Grief* (Fort Collins, Colo.: Center for Grief and Loss Recovery, 1991), 15.

3. Ibid., 20.

OBSERVE special days

1. Mary Higgins Clark, *Kitchen Privileges: A Memoir* (New York: Simon and Schuster, 2002), 116-17.

2. Grace Hyslop Christ, *Healing Children's Grief: Surviving a Parent's Death from Cancer* (New York: Oxford University Press, 2000), 56.

PLAY with the child

1. Joan Schweizer Hoff and Amy Lindholm, "The Needs of Children Impacted by Violent Death," *The Director* (2002, July), 57.

2. Kroen, *Helping Children Cope*, 41.

3. Fred Rogers, *The World According to Mr. Rogers* (New York: Hyperion, 2003), 183.

PRAY for and with the child

1. Alfred Lord Tennyson, "The Passing of Arthur," in Robert W. Hill Jr., ed., *Tennyson's Poetry: Authoritative Texts, Juvenilia and Early Responses, Criticism* (New York: Norton, 1971), 429.

2. Reed, *Mystery of Death*, 48.

3. Peter Fonda, *Don't Tell Dad* (New York: Hyperion, 1998), 45.

PLANT something

1. Kroen, *Helping Children Cope*, 78.

2. Wolfelt, *Healing a Child's Grieving Heart*, 67.

PRESERVE the past

1. Parish, *Rosie*, 4.

2. Michael Mayne, *Pray, Love, Remember* (London: Darton, Longman, and Todd, 1998), 58-59.

PROCESS media coverage

1. Michelle A. Beauchesne, Barbara R. Kelley, Carol A. Patsdaughter, and Jennifer Pickland (2002), "Attack on America: Children's Reactions and Parents' Responses," *Journal of Pediatric Healthcare*, 16(5), 216; 110.

QUESTION the child gently
1. Worden, *Children and Grief*, 149.

READ to or with the child
1. Lewis Carroll, *Alice's Adventures in Wonderland*, cited in John Bartlett, ed., *Familiar Quotations*, 15th ed. (Boston: Little, Brown, 1865), 611.
2. Sue Alexander, *Nadia the Willful* (New York: Pantheon Books, 1983), n.p.

RESPOND to the child's fears or anxieties
1. King, *Growing Up King*, 85.

RESIST the temptation to try to "make it all better"
1. Beauchesne, *Attack on America*, 221.
2. Condoleeza Rice, cited in Maria L. LaGanga, "In Race for White House, the 'Cult of Condi' Plays Growing Role," *Los Angeles Times* (May 28, 2000), A3.
3. Http://www.progressiveaustin.org/mlkeulogyu.htm
4. Condoleeza Rice, "Acknowledge That You Have an Obligation to Search for the Truth" (Address to the Graduating Class of Stanford University, June 16, 2002).

REMEMBER together
1. Rank, *Free to Grieve*, 133.

SEND cards
1. Suzanne C. Ryan, "Christmas Card Custom Under Stress," *Kansas City Star* (December 22, 1998), E6.
2. Shanna Bartlett Groves, "Greeting Cards Should Emphasize Quality, Not Quantity," *Kansas City Star* (December 14, 2003), D7.
3. Charmaine Caldwell, Marsha McGee, and Charles Pryor, "The Sympathy Card as Cultural Assessment of American Attitudes Toward Death, Bereavement and Extending Sympathy: A Replicated Study," *Omega* 37(2) (1998), 131.
4. Groves, "Greeting Cards," D7.

SHOW UP for special and routine events in the child's life
1. Young in Berry and Berry, *Reawakening to Life*, 88.

TALK about all kinds of things
1. Tener Goodwin Veenema and Kathryn Schroeder-Bruce, "The Aftermath of Violence: Children, Disaster, and Posttraumatic Stress Disorder," *Journal of Pediatric Health Care* 16(5) (2002), 243.

TELL the truth
1. Kroen, *Helping Children Cope*, 10.
2. Joy Johnson and Earl Grollman, *A Child's Book About Death* (Omaha: Centering Corporation, 2001), 14.
3. Kroen, *Helping Children Cope*, 29.
4. Hoff and Lindholm, *Needs of Children*, 57.

UTILIZE resources specifically designed for children
1. Brown and Brown, *When Dinosaurs Die*, inside flap.

VISIT the child
1. Jerry Falwell, *Strength for the Journey* (New York: Simon and Schuster, 1987), 85.

VISIT the cemetery or scattering area
1. Fitzgerald, *Grieving Child*, 100.
2. Ibid.

VALUE the child's faith wonderings
1. Ana Veciana-Suarez, *Birthday Parties in Heaven: Thoughts on Love, Life, Grief, and Other Matters of the Heart* (New York: Plume Books, 2000), 73.
2. Ibid.
3. Robert Benson, *Between the Dreaming and the Coming True* (San Francisco: HarperCollins, 1997), 48.

WRITE a poem or story or bumper sticker together
1. Susan Engel, *The Stories Children Tell: Making Sense of the Narratives of Childhood* (New York: W. H. Freeman, 1995/1999), 10.
2. Donna O'Tolle, "Storytelling with Children," in Nancy Boyd Webb, ed., *Helping Bereaved Children: A Handbook for Practitioners* (New York: Guilford Press, 2002), 323.
3. Wolfelt, *Healing a Child's Grieving Heart*, 14.
4. Wright, *It's Okay to Cry*, 87 (in manuscript format).
5. Worden, *Children and Grief*, 165.

WRITE a letter to the child
1. Andersen, *The Day John Died*, 75.

YOU can make a difference in this child's life
1. Fitzgerald, *Grieving Child*, 177.
2. Http://www.kirjasto.sci.fi/jmbarrie/htm
3. Laura Miller, "The Last Word: The Lost Boy," *New York Times Book Review* (December 14, 2003), 35.

ZOOM in on this child
1. Nuland, *Lost in America*, 85.
2. Charles A. Corr, "What Do We Know About Grieving Children and Adolescents?" In K. J. Doka, ed., *Living with Grief: Children, Adolescents, and Loss* (Philadelphia: Brunner/Mazel, 2000), 25.

Conclusion: A Tale of Two Children
1. Elizabeth Kubler-Ross, quoted in Fitzgerald, *Grieving Child*, 21-22.
2. John Toland, *The Dillinger Days* (New York: Da Capo Press, 1963/1995), 6.
3. Ibid.
4. Philip Yancey, *Disappointment with God: Three Questions No One Asks Aloud* (Grand Rapids: Zondervan, 1988), 311-12.
5. Rick Warren, *The Purpose-Driven Life: What on Earth Am I Here For?* (Grand Rapids: Zondervan, 2002), 141.
6. Abraham Lincoln, cited in Suzy Platt, ed., *Respectfully Quoted: A Dictionary of Quotations Requested from the Congressional Research Service* (Washington, D.C.: Library of Congress, 1989), 233.
7. Benjamin P. Thomas, *Abraham Lincoln* (New York: Knopf, 1952), 58.
8. Maude Shaw, "Now, John F. Kennedy's Children Go on Without Him," *Ladies Home Journal* (February 1966), 132.
9. Bush, *A Charge to Keep I Have*, 14.

Appendix A: Guidelines for Professional Evaluation of Grieving Children

1. Worden, *When Children Grieve*, 147-49.
2. Ibid., 149.

Appendix E: A Vocabulary for Talking About Death with Children

1. Lewis Carroll, cited in John Bartlett, *Familiar Quotations* (Boston: Little, Brown, and Company, 182), 613.